Being Successful in... Time Management

GW00372078

About the Author

As an independent consultant in the areas of management and organisation development, Tom also teaches at the Irish Management Institute where he runs programmes in organisation and management including time management. He has wide experience of working in the private and public sector and has worked on many overseas training and consulting assignments in Europe, the Middle and Far East and the United States.

In the early part of his career, Tom worked in business in the personnel, training and organisation development functions. He completed his Masters Degree in OD at Pepperdine University in Los Angeles and his Doctorate at Bath University.

Tom's interests include working as a process consultant with companies that are managing their own transitions. He also has an ongoing interest in helping managers improve their personal and interpersonal skills. He currently divides his time between consulting, teaching and writing.

Being Successful in...

Time Management

Tom McConalogue

BLACKHALL
Publishing

This book was typeset by Artwerk for

BLACKHALL PUBLISHING
26 Eustace Street
Dublin 2
Ireland

e-mail: blackhall@tinet.ie

ISBN: 1 901657 20 5

Printed in Ireland by
Betaprint Ltd

Series Foreword

The Being Successful in...series is a new series of practical books, which provides an accessible and user friendly approach to the common problems experienced by small to medium-sized, growing businesses.

The series will help businesses in the start-up phase but also covers problems encountered during the all-important development phase. It will be helpful to businesses which are starting to grow, and which need to cope with a range of unfamiliar, difficult and often competing issues.

The books in the series are comprehensive and yet concise, and they treat the topics in question succinctly and without recourse to jargon. Practical examples, checklists and pointers on to further sources of help and advice are included to supplement the text.

Books published in the *Being Successful in...series* in early 1999:

Being Successful in...Report Writing
Being Successful in...Customer Care
Being Successful in...Presentations
Being Successful in...Budgeting
Being Successful in...Patents, Copyright and Trade Marks

Forthcoming books in the series:

Being Successful in...Motivation
Being Successful in...Negotiations
Being Successful in...Market Research

Contents

Preface: Why You Should Read This Book

This is not another book of recipes on time management; we assume you have read those and are looking for something more. However, with all the current solutions on offer, such as personal organisers, computerised scheduling systems and electronic diaries, managers still continue to mismanage their time, not because they do not have remedies but because they lack the resolve to get started and make them work. Like the overweight person who may want to be thin but finds it hard to get into the diet, so managers find it hard to break the ingrained routines that trap them into a busy workstyle.

Time has become a more difficult resource to manage for two reasons. Firstly, the environment in which managers work has changed – while customers want instant response, and staff and colleagues are making more demands on their time, managers are also being challenged to improve service, quality, delivery and costs with less staff than before. All this has put pressure on managers to focus on the urgent and routine tasks and to work longer hours to keep pace with the increasing demands on their time, estimated by one survey as adding a month's work to their year over the last twenty years.

Secondly, time is becoming a more difficult resource for managers because of the way they respond to the increasing demands in their day. While the growth in office technology and information systems has helped managers to speed up their work flow, it has also lead to many being organised around the wrong things. By definition, managing is about getting things done for today, but it is also about making things happen for the future. As a manager it is all too easy to end up doing things right instead of doing the right things – busy organising the deck chairs on the sinking ship.

Efficiency is about doing things right.
Effectiveness is about doing the right things.
Excellence is about doing the right things right.

This book will tell you how to focus on the right things, how to find time for what is important in the job and how to let go of some of the routine and less important tasks. It will also suggest ways to tackle your bad habits with time and suggest better habits for using time more effectively as a resource.

And rather than another panacea on time management this book will offer you real choices to select what may work for you and the opportunity to develop those choices into practical actions.

Read on.

Chapter 1

Making Choices With Time

This chapter will help you to:

- establish the link between good management and making effective choices with time;

- identify the bad habits that may block you from being effective as a manager;

- develop good habits aimed at getting more direction and focus into what you do as a manager.

Making Choices With Time

Being effective as a manager is about making good choices with your time. Most of the problems managers have with time are the result from having many things to do and a limited amount of time in which to do them. So they have to make choices about which activities add most to their effectiveness and put the time where it belongs.

Managing time means choosing to do some things now and leaving other things until later, identifying some things as important and others as less important and acknowledging that some things are worth giving less of your time or not doing at all. But making those sometimes difficult decisions also creates stress – life was indeed simpler and less stressful when you had one suit and one breakfast cereal to choose from.

BAD HABITS AND STRESS

Under pressure from the many competing demands on their time, some managers avoid the stress that goes with making difficult choices by developing habits that are self-defeating and difficult to reverse. Managers typically get into four bad habits with their time.

> **WORD TO THE WISE**
> Hard work never killed anyone, but overwork killed many good horses.
> *Old Irish saying*

Trying to Do Everything

One of the ways in which managers cope with the pressure of time is by extending their day – coming in early, leaving late, grabbing a hurried lunch and taking work home. A recent report by the Institute of Management found over 38 per cent of managers working more than 50 hours a week and 41 per cent regularly taking work home at the weekends.

Not only does working long hours become a habit (many managers would not know what to do with themselves if they went home on time), it is also a vain attempt to get everything done in the day. The well established principle in Parkinson's law that "work expands to fill the available time", also reminds us that no matter how many hours in the day there will never be enough time to get everything done. Working long hours to beat your way out of over commitment and time pressure is not very skilful – any old fool can work hard – but neither is it managing, it is being managed.

Focusing on Urgency

A second habit managers develop, in an attempt to get more control of their time, is to favour urgency over importance. In the typical working day, many things are urgent but only a few things are really that important. God forbid, if any one of us were knocked down in the road tomorrow, most of what we do would be picked up by somebody else, or might not get done at all with very little consequence. It supports a view that the manager's contribution lies in the few important things they achieve in their day, not in the volume of routine and urgency they handle. But, in the typical working day the important things often get done last rather than first, or they are completed outside working hours when managers have least energy for thinking or planning.

Focusing on the immediate and urgent tasks, rather than on what is important, sees many managers drifting effortlessly into the "activity trap" where crisis and reaction dictate the workload

rather than being driven by the managers own aspirations and challenges in the job.

Hanging on to the Routine

A third habit that managers develop under pressure
from time is retreating into routine work which provides them with some comfort that they are indeed
getting things done. Routine meetings, correspondence, reports, paperwork and appointments are
examples of the kind of work that managers are only
too willing to commit time to without thinking about
the contribution it makes to their effectiveness. Many
managers spend the first and most important chunk
of their day on tasks that may be necessary but are
also part of the comfort zone, like opening the post,
checking e-mail, responding to telephone messages
or following up on post-it notes. Do you enjoy getting
back to the office after a holiday or a business trip to
find messages, e-mail and post-it notes to relax you
into the first couple of hours? Be honest.

Much of the routine work in a manager's day is
at best work they should be giving to others, work
they should be giving less of their time or work
they should not be doing at all. Yet managers continue to occupy themselves with a great deal of
routine and trivia in their day either because it is,
familiar work, which they do not want to let go, or
because it serves as a convenient alibi for not getting into the more challenging and difficult parts of
the job.

Saying "Yes" instead of "No"

How often have you come away from a meeting only
to kick yourself for having said "yes" to something.
Over 70 per cent of managers admit to saying "yes"
far too often and recognise the need be more
assertive with their time.

Saying "yes" when you should be saying "no" is a

habit that comes from two sources. Under pressure it is often easier and less stressful to say "yes" to things, particularly if they are somewhere in the future. If a colleague asked you to do something in three weeks time you would probably say "yes", while if the same colleague asked you to drop everything and give them an hour of your time right now your answer would probably be more thoughtful.

Saying "yes" is also a product of not having clear direction in your job. If you do not have priorities to which you are committing chunks of time in your day it is much more difficult to say "no" to the demands of others. Alternatively, if you are committed to getting a report completed in the next two days or planning a new schedule by lunch time it is much easier to say "no" to people. And saying "no" does not mean turning down every request, but it does mean making choices that are based on the most effective use of your time and not regretting the sometimes ill-considered decisions that waste your time.

Figure 1.1: Symptoms and Bad Habits

Rate the following symptoms as:
A big problem-2, problem-1, no problem-0

1. Working long hours or taking work home.
2. Feeling of overwork or pressure in the job.
3. Always urgency and crises in the job.
4. Not giving enough time to the major priorities.
5. Time taken on paperwork and routine administration.
6. Doing routine work that could be done by others.
7. Not saying "no" often enough.
8. Responding to many demands from customers, colleagues or staff.

Add your marks:

1+2 Doing too much.

2+4 Focusing on urgency.

5+6 Hanging on to the routine.

7+8 Saying "yes" too often.

Many of the work habits that managers develop to cope with time pressures in the job are self-defeating in the short-term and habitual in the longer term. And, like most bad habits, they are hard to break because managers get comfortable with working long hours, responding to urgency and over committing themselves. While some managers grudgingly admit to being stressed and overworked, many have an investment in their illness as well as in the cure because it allows them to justify their ineffectiveness to themselves and attracts sympathy from others. But ask yourself this: "To what degree are my time problems caused by the situation in which I am managing, or have I just drifted into working this way?" While there are some things that managers have little option but to get done, much of the way they use their time is guided by habit or by choice.

MAKING BETTER CHOICES

Although time is like any other resource, such as money, people or equipment, it is a difficult resource to manage and an almost impossible one to control. Not only is it totally perishable, you cannot save an hour today and use it tomorrow when you might be busy, but time is always in short supply. If you reduced the number of hours in your day by the amount of time you spend dealing with minor issues, on things to which you should have said "no", the time spent on work you should have given to others and on dealing with interruptions, then you are left with no more than two or three really productive hours in the average day. Respected commentators, such as Peter Drucker, Edward Demming and Gareth Morgan, all agree that managers have less than 25 per cent of their time under their control and the only way to use that precious resource wisely is to ensure that your choices are guided by what you want to get done instead of letting others make those choices for you.

Habit 1: Know Where the Hours are Going

The place to start managing yourself is not with what you want to do with your time but how you are using it right now. Most managers over and under-estimate the amount of time they give to their major tasks by at least 50 per cent and most people could not account for how they spent yesterday, never mind last week. The shortage of data on where their time actually goes is a major block to managers who want to make better and more informed choices for the future.

Habit 2: Keep the End in Mind

As the saying predicts: "If you do not know where you are going, you may end up somewhere else." By definition, managing is not just about doing things for today, it is also about implementing things, changing things, improving things and developing things for the future.

While most managers have an appreciation of their strategic functions, they also find it remark-ably easy to fill their day with activity that has little to do with managing the future. And apart from finding your own sense of direction in the job, it is much easier to get others to share the journey if they too are inspired by your hopes and dreams for the future.

Habit 3: Work to the Priorities

Many managers end up giving away their effectiveness by assuming that everything is of equal importance. Yet ask any manager to list their key tasks in the job and few have a problem identifying the four or five activities that stand out well above the rest.

While it almost goes without saying that having priorities at work is a good thing, the main issue is finding time to manage them. Many managers who have clear and challenging priorities end up giving them very little of their time – less than 10 per cent for most managers according to Henry Mintzberg. Apart from having longer term priorities to provide you with a sense of direction, it is also important to find disciplines for working on them daily and weekly to ensure that you focus on the things you want to make happen as well as the things that need to get done.

Habit 4: Schedule Time for the Important Things

Priorities are a function of what you pay attention to, by giving them time. If you say that something is a priority and you are not giving it solid chunks of your day or week, then by definition it is not a priority. Likewise, many things get done if you simply make time for them, like developing relationships, passing exams or getting fit. While it is easy for managers to excuse their lack of achievement by saying "I didn't have the time" or "I have been under pressure", like most people they can always find time for the things they really want to do, like an overseas conference or a golf outing. The way you establish things as priorities is by making time for them, whether by blocking out hours in your diary, using a 'to do' list or institutionalising them as regular commitments for particular days or weeks.

Habit 5: Delegate Routine and Responsibility

Getting more time for the important things in your

job also means letting go of some of the less important things, either by getting your staff more involved in handling the routine work, developing procedures for handling recurring problems, or empowering your people to take more risks, make mistakes and learn from them. Most managers could also let go of an amount of paperwork, meetings or problem solving by giving those things less of their time or pushing them back to those who should be dealing with them in the first place. Making a habit of dealing with the most important things first is also a way of relegating the least important things to times of the day where many of them belong.

Habit 6: Confront your Indecision and Delay

Most people procrastinate on certain things, whether finishing a report, completing staff appraisals or dealing with a problem person. However, procrastination and indecision can also become habits when managers, through fear of failure, do not start them at all or wait for a crisis to spur them into action. Confronting the anxiety, which accompanies indecision and procrastination, means finding ways to see them as manageable challenges rather than as opportunities to fail.

Habit 7: Minimise the Daily Distractions

The typical manager's day is fragmented by interruption from the telephone, visitors, minor problems and ad hoc meetings. While they only take a few minutes here and there, the cumulative effect of time wasters can add up to a massive block to getting things done. Though you may not be able to get rid of time wasters altogether, because many of them go with the job, you could start to manage the effects of interruption on your day by recognising the extent to which you collude or even encourage the things about which you complain. Enjoy some of the time wasters for what they are, part of the buzz of the job, and find ways to manage the others by minimising them or controlling their effects on getting the important things done.

Habit 8: De-stress the Work Pressure

While there is nothing wrong with the kind of stress that accompanies a tight deadline or crisis, it is mainly the negative side of work pressure that managers recognise in themselves. With symptoms, such as anxiety, interrupted sleep, lack of concentration and digestive problems, many of the habits that managers develop to cope with the effects of work pressure, such as long hours, coffee, cigarettes or self-medication, simply add to those symptoms.

Two broad approaches to stress management emphasise the importance of building time into your day for relaxation on the basis that managing is a stressful activity, and in the longer term by developing habits to reduce or eliminate the root causes of stress.

Habit 9: Start to Make it Happen

Many of the common responses to time pressure in the job are developed in a manager's early career when he/she is striving for recognition and promotion and learning from the bad habits of others. Although some habits serve a function in dealing with short-term crises and urgency, they frequently persist well beyond their usefulness, and only in later career do many managers regret how much time they gave to some things and how little to others. How many managers later in their careers will regret that they did not take enough care of their health or spend more time with their families? How many will recognise their long hours as having blocked them from achieving other things in their lives? How many managers on their deathbeds will regret that they did not spend enough time in the office?

Managing time means accepting that you have little choice about doing some things but that many others are within your control. As well as looking for better ways to organise your 'busyness', start to challenge some of the behaviours that get in the way of what you really want to achieve with your time. Learn to unblock the bad habits that may be sustaining an unhealthy work style or preventing you from getting more satisfaction from managing. Get more mileage from your efforts by focusing on the things you really want to make happen and scheduling time for those things. Do something to let go of one of your major time wasters or get more balance in your personal life. If you do not start to manage your time it can easily end up controlling you.

God, grant me the serenity to accept the things I cannot change,

The courage to change the things I can,

And the wisdom to know the difference.

REMEMBER

DO:

- Control the controllable – accept that some things have to be done but that many things are a choice.

- Rather then trying to do everything in the day, start to make wiser choices with your time.

- Develop good habits that help you focus on the important things and let go of the urgency, routine and time wasters in the job.

DO NOT:

- Kill your effectiveness as a manager by focusing on urgency at the expense of importance.

Chapter 2

Know Where The Hours Are Going

This chapter will help you to:

- recognise that the place to start making more effective use of your time is by understanding where it is going;

- identify ways to get data on where your time is currently going and should be going for the future;

- understand how managers get drawn into the operating side of the job at the expense of the managerial and strategic side of their function.

Know Where The Hours Are Going

When managers first experience problems with their time, the immediate response is to look for a panacea, whether a new diary, a personal organiser, a resolution to start working differently or a demand for additional staff. Isn't that one of the reasons you bought this book – to look for solutions?

Imagine, however, that you had a weight problem and went along to a fitness centre for help. Would they start by telling you to go on a crash diet, to follow an exercise plan or to cut out certain foods from your rations? No, they would probably begin by giving you a fitness test, measuring and weighing you, or enquiring about your current diet. They know that the place you start with changing personal habits is not with solutions but with data. Understanding what is happening in your life, and the options for doing things differently is the key to changing most things for the future.

One of the major obstacles to changing our personal habits with time is that managers do not have even the most basic of data on where their time actually goes. Most managers could not give a decent account of how they spent yesterday and few have more than a hazy idea of what they did with last week. Added to that, managers, like most people, are poor judges of time, underestimating the hours needed to get most things done by at least 50 per cent, never budgeting enough time for the important jobs and assuming that their staff can do things in half the time required. It should be of real concern today that many businesses which profess to have such tight controls on their other resources, such as materials, money and equipment, have so little information on what their managers and staff are doing with their time.

THE 'BUSYNESS' TRAP

> **WORD TO THE WISE**
> What is the point of doing things efficiently that do not need be done in the first place?

Like most people, managers are poor judges of time because their experience relates to what they are doing – time speeds up when you are doing things that you enjoy doing and slows down when you are doing things you dislike. Simplifying the concept of relativity, Albert Einstein once suggested that it was like "being in the company of a beautiful woman for a minute of time and sitting on top of a red hot fire for the same length of time – it's a different experience". Although we measure time as if it were a constant, in reality it speeds up and slows down as we go through the day.

> With the aid of a timer or watch, and sitting in a comfortable position, try to judge a minute of your time. Resist the temptation to start counting, just try to feel the minute. When you think the minute is up, check the timer and see how far your estimate is out. Most people under or overestimate a minute by at least fifteen seconds.

Confused about where their time is going, and feeling they are not getting enough from all the hours they are putting into the job is an inducement for many managers to work even harder to beat their way out of over commitment. Rather than looking at what they are doing with their time, managers often retreat into 'busyness' and overwork on the basis that, if you do not know where you are going at least you can look good. Unfortunately, for many managers, looking good often means drifting into habits that are hard to break, such as long hours, taking work home and an over concern for the routine and trivia.

Managing time is not about getting more things

done with your day, it is a process for finding ways to focus on the important things and avoiding the activity trap. The place to start the process is with looking at where your time is going right now as the best guide to where it should go for the future. While there are simple ways to account for your time on a daily or weekly basis, it is useful now and again to carry out a more thoughtful review of your time by keeping a log, reviewing your diary or touching base with your feelings and frustrations about time.

Keep a Time Log

A periodic review of your time does not have to be a complicated exercise, but if you feel under constant pressure from time, or are getting less than you expect from the hours you put into the job, then consider keeping a simple record of your time over a couple of typical working days.

Figure 2.1: Time Log

		P.	D.	W.	O/M
8.30-8.45	Checking daily work	✔			M
8.45-9.00	Opening post		✔		O
9.00-9.15	Answering correspondence		✔	✔	O
9.15-9.30	Responding to queries		✔		O
9.30-9.45	Responding to queries		✔	✔	O
9.45-10.00	Production meeting			✔	M
10.00-10.15	Production meeting			✔	O
10.15-10.30	Production meeting	✔			O
10.30-10.45	MBWA	✔			M
10.45-11.00	Meeting John re:invoice		✔		O
		30	50	40	30

Take a sheet of lined paper and identify each line as a 1/4 hour in your working day. Over the next day or two, write down what you are doing in each quarter of an hour as you are doing it. Complete the record as close to the time as possible and do not leave it beyond an hour. When you get to the end of the day, add up the total number of 1/4 hours you worked on that day.

Now analyse the data under four simple headings.

1. **Priorities**. In the first column go down through the activities each quarter of an hour and identify which were priorities on that day – priorities are tasks that made a significant contribution to what you were trying to achieve, not the things that had to be done or took a lot of your time. Be ruthless in identifying the real priorities, they are by definition a few rather than many things. Now add up the number of 1/4 hours you spent on priority activities that day and percentage it over the total number of quarter hours available.

2. **Delegation**. In the second column, again go down the list for each 1/4 of an hour and identify the delegatable activities – those tasks you could or should have given to someone else to complete – including the priority activities. You may find that although you could not delegate a whole task you could have given part of it to someone else. As well as the tasks you could have given to others, also consider tasks you could have let go by saying "no" or giving less of your time. Now add up the number of quarter hours you spent on *D's* and percentage it over the total.

3. **Time Wasters**. Next, go down through the list and identify the time you spent dealing with interruptions on that day. Include the things that distracted you from what you were trying to get done or where you should have said "no". Time wasters are sometimes difficult to identify because many of them are part of the job, it is only when they eat into the major tasks or start to affect your ability to manage your day, that they become a waste. Again, add up the number of *Ws* and percentage it over the total.

4. **Operating and Managing**. In the final column go down through the list of activities and identify them as managing or operating work – put an *O* or an *M* beside each 1/4 hour. Although there is an element of greyness between managing and operating work, *managing* activities relate to "achieving results through other people", such as planning, delegating work or reviewing results. Conversely the *operating* tasks are the technical/professional part of your job or the routine work which could be done by others. Again add up the time you spent on operating work and managing work and find the percentage balance.

Having completed the analysis ask yourself a few questions, or better still write half a page of commentary.

- What kind of day was it: effective or busy?
- What was good or disappointing about your time on that day?
- How typical was it of a normal working day?
- What is the data telling you about the way in which you currently use your time and could use it better?

Keeping a time log over a couple of typical working days is always revealing, sometimes reassuring and often disturbing. Managers who keep a log, are usually surprised at how little time they spend on the real priorities, or how the priorities got side-tracked by the volume of routine work or urgent tasks. Also revealing is that much of the work on which managers spend their time could be delegated to others, if they gave consideration to clarifying people's jobs and allocated more responsibility to their key staff. And, typically, an average of 20 per cent of the manager's day is wasted by distractions, which fragment their day and eat into the major priorities.

Figure 2.2: Key Task Analysis

Tasks	M	T	W	T	F	Tot

A simpler variation of the time log involves listing down the 4-8 key tasks in your job and tracking the time you give them over the next week, indicating in hours or parts of an hour how much you spend on each activity. The simple action of tracking your time on the important activities is often enough to start changing them.

Review your Diary

One permanent record of where managers commit their time is a diary. While diaries can be a useful tool in scheduling for the future, they are also part of the time trap for managers who frequently use them to record commitments they should never have agreed to in the first place. Managers also get some comfort from having a full diary, which relieves them from having to do anything except look to their diary and religiously follow those commitments. Not only do managers commit time to others at the expense of their own priorities, but a full diary is often used as an excuse for their lack of effectiveness in the day.

One of the ways to get convincing data on specific activities, such as meetings, visits, travel, presentations, networking or appointments, is to analyse the last three to six months of your diary. Use this analysis to identify the tasks that take up a lot of your time and those for which you may need to schedule more time.

As Director in a social services organisation, Alan spends a great deal of his time at meetings, some regular and some ad hoc, some internal and others with outside agencies. Feeling, that he was just rushing from one meeting to another prompted him to count up the hours he spent at meetings over the past six months and to categorise them into external and internal, regular, ad hoc and team meetings. The analysis revealed that he was spending a staggering 60 hours a month at outside meetings and less than three hours a month with his own staff. He set a goal to reduce the time spent at external meetings by twenty hours a month through attending some of them intermittently and delegating others to his staff. He also set a goal to spend six hours a week with his staff to include monthly 'one-on-ones' and a weekly meeting. Now, at the end of each week, he reviews his diary against those two goals and reschedules his time accordingly.

As a part of the analysis, compare the hours you spent on major diaried activities in the past six months with the total hours in your week or the amount of time you gave to other activities. When counting up the hours on activities, such as meetings or visits, also include the travel and preparation time involved.

GET IN TOUCH WITH YOUR FEELINGS

Apart from analysing a time log or your diary commitments, do not ignore the data on how you feel about your time – sometimes the soft data is the most compelling for change – your stress level, confusion about your role, the constant pressure or just feeling out of control with your time.

One way to get some data on your feelings is to take five minutes each evening to write a brief reflection on the day: What you achieve? What frustrated your efforts? What will you resolve to do differently tomorrow? If a daily reflection sounds too much then do it weekly on a Friday as a part of planning for next week. Alternatively, at times you feel under pressure take five minutes to get those feelings down on paper as a way of reducing your anxiety and getting more certainty about the cause.

Also involve others in the process of sensing out the soft data by getting their views on aspects of your work style that may be helping or frustrating your efforts. As well as getting personal feedback from your staff, also get them to reflect on where their time is going. Managers often end up being overworked and unsupported because they are reluctant to overload their busy staff with even more work – so they do it themselves. But, ask yourself this: "What are your staff busy doing?" If they analysed their time they would probably find much of it is taken up with minor routines and urgent tasks that could be reduced or eliminated. Also, remind yourself that it is their job to assist in achieving your results as a manager, and if you are frustrated about the level of assistance you are getting, it is most likely because they see their job and priorities differently.

WHAT MANAGERS REALLY DO WITH TIME

As one of your most critical resources in the job, the only way to get more control of your time is to spend

it wisely on the things that contribute most to your effectiveness.
Data from over 60 diary and obser-
vational studies reveals a disturbing
picture, confirming a view that
many businesses today are over-
administrated and under-managed.

• Managers Give Very Little Time to their Priorities

Although, by definition, management is about achieving results, managers spend less than 10 per cent of
their day on the things they identify as priorities in
the job. Rather than giving concentrated chunks of
time to what they see as important, their time tends
to be fragmented and unfocused, driven by routine
and urgency, and they seem to enjoy it that way.

• Few Managers Have a Daily, Weekly or Long-term Plan

While some of the time that managers spend reacting to crises is caused by other people, much of it
reflects their own lack of planning. Few managers
spend even five minutes in the morning planning
what they want to get out of the day. Instead they
look to their diary for inspiration or busy themselves with routines, such as the post or e-mail,
until the first meeting or interruption sets them on
course for the rest of the day.

SOME FACTS

• Less than 10 per cent of the manager's day
is spent on priority tasks.

• Managers spend less than 30 per cent of
their time on managerial tasks.

- Managers are interrupted on average every 7 minutes.

- 90 per cent of the manager's time is spent on activities of less than 9 minutes.

- 36-69 per cent of the manager's time is spent at meetings.

- Thinking time for manager's is less than 5 per cent of their day.

- Senior managers spend less than 3 per cent of their time on strategic issues.

In the longer term, few managers have a monthly plan, long-term goals or a vision for the future. Yet ask any manager what they need to make more time for and – surprise, surprise – planning always comes top of the list.

• Managers are Constantly Interrupted

One of the most common excuses for lack of achievement in the job is the volume of interruptions that come at the manager each day. With an average of one interruption every seven minutes from the telephone, drop in visitors, paperwork or minor crises, managers get the important things done in between the interruptions.

Although they may only take a few minutes here and there, interruptions account for up to 25 per cent of the manager's day, not only making it difficult for them to give concentrated time to their major tasks but forcing them to do the most important things at times of the day they have least energy for planning or thinking.

• Managers Spend Little Quality Time with their Staff

Although up to 30 per cent of managers' time is spent with staff, most of it is reacting to the immediate problems and issues of the day. Managers give very little time to training staff, reviewing their performance or counselling and developing people. As a consequence, they end up doing many things themselves that could be done by their staff if they were better informed and more competent.

While it is argued by some commentators that today's environment requires managers to be flexible to the changing demands of the economy, an opposing view is that overwork and stress are symptoms of managers not having adapted to an environment which demands that they focus on the important things and let go of the trivia that can so easily fill their day. The solution probably lies somewhere in the balance, that to remain responsive managers have to be flexible to the immediate issues while at the same time remaining clearly focused on the future. Total flexibility, without plan or direction, is a recipe for chaos and under-achievement while being totally focused and over-scheduled can lead managers to being inflexible and bureaucratic.

What is certain today is that managers are under increasing pressure from a variety of demands on their time. The only way to retain a healthy balance between what needs to be done for today and what needs to be made happen for the future is to develop good habits with your time and control the bad habits that can so easily lead to long hours, stress and over commitment. At the beginning of that journey, more important than solutions, is a better understanding of where your time is going and needs to go for the future.

REMEMBER

DO:

- Keep a time log periodically to check on your use of time.

- Review your diary and plan to reduce your commitments to other people.

- Avoid over commitment by giving yourself time to make the right choices.

- Start having meetings and appointments with yourself.

DO NOT:

- Look for solutions until you understand the problems with your time.

Chapter 3

Keep The End In Mind

This chapter will help you to:

- clarify your direction for the future with a vision and clear challenges in the job;
- find ways to come down from your aspirations to goals for action;
- fuel your long-term challenges with energy for the journey.

Keep The End In Mind

Did you hear the story of the airline pilot who announced to the passengers that he had some good news and some bad news. "The good news is we are doing over 600 miles an hour – the bad news is that we're lost." As a manager, you may share similar feelings of being busily engaged on the wrong things, working hard rather than going anywhere.

Not only is overwork and lack of direction a recipe for under achievement, it is also a common source of stress for managers. In a recent interview to promote *The Little Book of Calm*, author Paul Wilson identified the two most common sources of job stress as overwork and being out of control with your time. While hard work can be both challenging and energising, if it is leading somewhere, without direction or purpose it simply adds to the feelings of being out of control: as Thomas Carlyle once proclaimed "there is nothing more terrifying than activity without insight".

What makes time a complex and difficult resource to manage is that there are often competing demands between what has to be done for today and what needs to be done for the future. Although managers are expected to handle the day to day tasks efficiently, they are also expected to achieve results in the longer term; to improve things, to innovate and to develop things. Yet the overwhelming pressure in most organisations is for managers to be reactive rather than strategic. As a consequence the challenge of managing is absent for many, reflected in one survey that identifies more than 78 per cent of managers as being dissatisfied with their jobs, having, low in self-esteem and, if they had a choice, wanting to pursue an alternative career – so much for the rewards of managing.

CREATING THE CHALLENGE

A career in plastic surgery lead Dr Maxwell Maltz to
identify a clear link between self-esteem and challenge in life. In a book entitled *Psycho-cybernetics*,
he recalls how many of the patients who came to his
clinic hoped in some way that a change in their
physical appearance would change their lives. He
found that although surgery worked in a positive
way for some patients, for many others it did little
to change the way they saw themselves – those who
felt good about themselves before surgery continued
to feel good afterwards, and those who felt they were
failures continued to behave as if they still had an
ugly face or a physical disability. Concluding that
self-esteem comes from what we do in our lives
rather than how we see ourselves, he suggests that
man is like a bicycle, maintaining his poise and
equilibrium only so long as he is going forward
towards something.

> ...man is engineered as a goal seeking mecha-
> nism, built to conquer the environment, solve
> problems, achieve goals, and we find no real
> satisfaction and happiness in life without
> obstacles to conquer and goals to achieve.
>
> *Dr Maxwell Maltz*

The extent to which managers set and meet challenges in the job is also important in defining how
they see themselves as managers. While some feel
overworked and out of control with their time, others'
with a clearer sense of what they are trying to
achieve, see the same constraints as challenges to
succeed. Meeting those challenges not only helps
them grow in confidence as managers, it encourages
them to set even more ambitious challenges for the

future – as Thomas Huxley once wrote: "The rung of a ladder was never meant to rest upon, but only to hold a mans foot long enough to put it somewhere higher."

In summary, the way you act determines how you see yourself and as you see yourself, so you act. The way to become a self-confident and effective manager is to start behaving like one.

GET A LIFE: GET A VISION

You may have heard the tale of the traveller who came across three artisans cutting stone in a small quarry. Out of curiosity he asks them in turn what they are doing. The first who is idling against a wall says, "I am doing what I am told to do." Another, who is cleaning his implements, says, "I am just cutting stone." He moves on to the third who, though busy at work looks up to inform the traveller, "I am building a cathedral." While it is sometimes easier to settle for the routine or operational side of the job, the benefits of having clear long-term challenges is that it gives purpose to what you are trying to do as a manager. In addition to providing direction to your own efforts, a clear vision is also important in the process of leading others towards a better future and an antidote to the ever present activity trap.

> **WORD TO THE WISE**
> If you do not know where you are going, any road will get you there.

One way of getting in touch with your aspirations and challenges as a manager is by "looking out" at the environment and "looking in" at your values and vision for the future.

Looking Out
Organisations today are much more conscious of the environment than they were ten years ago and many

businesses get into trouble because they ignore the competition, new technology and changes in consumer demand. Healthy organisations and effective managers anticipate the changes that are likely to affect their area for the future and see them as challenges to improve things, to change things and to grow the business.

Take a moment to consider the changing environment in your area for the next year or two. What challenges does it present?

- **Technology**: new or modified, changing attitudes and uses, user-friendliness, customer expectation.

- **Consumer demand**: for better quality, service, design, ease of use, instant response, cheaper products and services, variety.

- **Competition**: more choice of supplier, cost cutting, new entrants, bigger competitors.

- **Legislation**: social, environmental, medical, working hours, conditions.

- **Labour market**: structure, availability, better qualified, more expectation.

- **Markets**: changes in distribution, demographics, age structure, sophistication.

- **Innovation**: speed, new materials, investment, new systems, processes, markets.

Figure 3.1: External Challenges

Identify three external challenges for your area over the next two to three years. What responses are you currently making to them? What would be a more proactive response for the next year?

	Challenges	Current Response	Better Response
1			
2			
3			

Looking In

Getting clearer direction for the future is also helped by revisiting your personal values and vision. Ask yourself a few basic questions about who you are as a manager and where you want to go for the next 1-2 years

- What do you want to give more time or take on as challenges? For example, better teamwork, more openness, greater flexibility, more training.

- Where do you want to be in a years time that is a better place than now? For example, a new system in place, new markets for existing products, doubling of staff, clear market leader.

- Where do you want to go with your values for the next year? For example, develop a customer service programme, reduce overheads, get ISO, make changes in work practices or participation.

- Which of these do you identify as a challenge for the next 1-2 years?
  1. Increased market share, revenue and productivity.

2. Better on-time delivery.
3. Improved customer service, customer retention.
4. Better teamwork and integration.
5. Increased team spirit.
6. Better morale and motivation.
7. More flexible and empowered staff.
8. Culture of continuous improvement.
9. Achieving a standard, e.g. ISO, quality mark, excellence through people.
10. Reduced waste, downtime, rejects, complaints or overtime.
11. New products and services.
12. Better trained staff.
13. Any others.

Figure 3.2: SWOT Analysis

A systematic way of identifying the challenges in your area is to carry out a SWOT Analysis. Take a sheet of paper and divide it into four boxes. In each of the boxes brainstorm a list of the Internal Strengths (S) and Weaknesses (W) and the External Opportunities (O) and Threats (T). Even better, do the exercise with your team – all it needs is a flip chart and an hour or two.

When you have completed the brainstorm (about ten minutes per box) from each box identify one thing you intend to take on as a challenge for the next year.

	Internal		External	
S	Quality Products, Good Service, Customer Base	New Technologies, Changing Demographics, Educated Customers	O
W	Lack of Trained Staff, Inadequate Systems, Weak Supervisor	Tighter Legislation, New Competitors, Cheap imports	T

Turn Your Aspirations into Goals

While a clear fix on the environment and a vision for the future can give you a better sense of where you are going, many of the things that managers want to make happen for the long-term are broad and aspirational, such as improving the product range, better teamwork, shorter lead times or increased market share. As such, they are hard to action because they sound like New Year's resolutions – and we all know how long *they* last. It helps generate commitment to your future aspirations if you make them into SMART goals – Specific, Measurable, Agreed, Realistic and Time bound.

Figure 3.3: Vision into Tasks

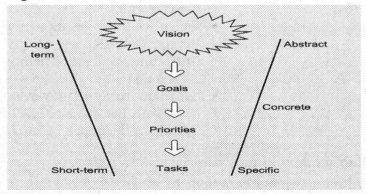

Turning aspirations into goals is as old as God's command to Noah to: "Build an Ark 30 cubits long and 30 cubits wide in seven months and to take on board a male and a female of every animal." In more recent history, when the NASA Space Agency was losing ground to Russian technology, Kennedy gave them new life by articulating the space programme as a goal: "To get a man on the moon and safely back to earth by the end of the decade." Not only do goals provide a clear challenge to succeed, they also make the seemingly impossible things possible. For thirteen years the 4-minute mile appeared beyond the reach of athletes until Roger Bannister broke the barrier on 6 May 1954 in a time of 3.59.4 minutes. In the following year over thirteen runners broke the magical 4-minute mile.

Take a little time to identify some medium-term goals for the next six to twelve months that will move you in the direction of your vision. Draw up a list of things you could do and select two or three of them for action.

Vision: 3 years

- Build an effective team of multi-skilled sales staff to achieve an 80 per cent customer service rating by 30 November.

Goals: 1 year

- Train all staff in customer service skills.
- Have regular 2 monthly team meetings.
- Introduce a team briefing system.
- Have quarterly job reviews.
- Deal with the three problem people in the department.

Light Many Fires

Although goals can help to make aspirations more concrete, ultimately you keep your aspirations alive by what you do on a daily and a weekly basis. Start the process by having your goals in writing as a constant reminder that you are there to achieve things for the future as well as work hard.

> **WORD TO THE WISE**
> In the absence of goals and priorities for the future, the fallback position is day to day 'busyness'.

Involve your staff in creating the goals, or at least share them with your staff, and make sure they are frequently on the agenda of your staff meetings.

Other ways to keep your goals alive includes

committing dates to your diary when you expect to have them completed, using slogans to capture the spirit of a goal, setting up task groups to manage them, constantly repeating them to others as a way of reminding yourself, and finding many ways to walk the walk.

Feargal Quinn has built a formidable reputation for the supermarket chain Superquinn through his commitment to customer service. Based on the "boomerang principle", the challenge is to provide such a good experience for shoppers that will return again and again. As part of that process, he does many things to fuel the challenge, through slogans such as: "You came for the prices and stayed for the service", comprehensive staff induction, continuous training, innovations (e.g. bread shops, umbrellas on wet days and assistance for mothers who are shopping for their children). He regularly packs groceries, meets with his suppliers on the floor so they can hear directly from customers and has focus groups where customers are encouraged to complain and contribute to improvements. In a variety of other ways too, such as giving managers tie pins with the letters YCDBSOYA – "you can't do business sitting on your ass" – he reminds his staff that customer service means everyone walking the walk.

Make an appointment with yourself each month to check your progress on your long-term goals – diarise it as a solid commitment so it happens. Also diarise an annual commitment to revisit the environment or your values and vision for the future. Complete a SWOT analysis once a year with your staff or involve them in reviewing your values, which inevitably decay unless they are constantly renewed. Review your values annually by rating them against your practice.

> At Intel, managers are rated once a year by their staff on how well they managed the values, such as risk taking, customer orientation and making it a great place to work. Every McDonald's outlet is audited annually on their management of the core values of quality, cleanliness and service.

Few managers ever attempt to verbalise their aspirations and goals in the job almost for fear that expressing them could deny their achievement. However, by not having a clear sense of where you are going for the future, you run the risk of succeeding at just one thing – being busy. A great deal of energy is available to managers from examining where they want to go and what they want to achieve. Only by having a clear sense of direction can you hope to avoid the drift into short efficiency at the expense of longer term effectiveness – remember the saying: "If you don't know where you are going you may end up somewhere else."

REMEMBER

DO:

- Remember that apart from getting things done for today, you should be doing things for the future.

- Get direction and energy for the future by having a vision of where you want to go as a manager.

- Make your aspirations and ambitions into concrete challenges by converting them into goals.

Chapter 4

Focus On The Priorities

This chapter will help you to:

- distinguish between the reactive and proactive side of your job;

- set and work to priorities by breaking them into tasks;

- keep sight of your priorities on a daily and weekly basis.

Focus On The Priorities

While having a vision for the future helps to give you direction as a manager, many people with clear ambitions and aspirations in life never achieve any of them. How many people who say they have a book to write ever see it published? How many with ambitions to change their careers, get a further qualification, travel the world, get promoted, own their own business or live in another culture ever achieve their ideals? Look back at your early career and life-time ambitions. How many have you realised so far?

PROACTIVE AND REACTIVE WORK

The main barrier to turning aspirations into achievements, is that managers have two competing demands on their time. On one side is the operational part of the job, which includes routine meetings, paperwork, problem solving and interruptions, and on the other they also have to manage the broader responsibilities, such as meeting targets, achieving deadlines, developing their area and completing projects. Although they often complain about the amount of routine and reaction in their day, managers by and large do not have a problem with that type of work which gets done because it is tangible, short-term and familiar – in fact managers enjoy much of it. What managers have much more difficulty finding time for is the proactive side of the job, which is long-term and much less demanding of their immediate attention. In the normal course of events, as Gresham's law states, "routine and urgency tends to drive out the important work".

The essential difference between managing the

day to day operational work and focusing on key tasks, such as developing staff or introducing new services, is that reactive work is largely driven by events and other people, while proactive work has to be made to happen. Apart from the practical difficulties of finding time and energy to make the bigger things happen, there is a great deal of organisational pressure on managers to be responsive and short-term in their thinking – often they report to bosses who want instant reaction and quick results – and what gets rewarded generally gets done.

Figure 4.1: The Reactive/Proactive Balance

Reactive Work	**Proactive Work**
Handling daily routines	Developing the area
Dealing with urgency	Focusing on key tasks
Resolving crises	Achieving deadlines and targets
Handling interruptions	Managing projects
Getting things done	Making things happen

The only way for managers to ensure that they are not overwhelmed by their day to day work is to have clear challenges in the job and to find ways of getting as energised about the future as they are about the present. There are two important ingredients in being proactive as a manager, firstly knowing what you want to make happen and secondly finding the energy to get started and keep going when things get tough. While getting direction for the future is partly a function of having long-term aspirations, it also helps to have shorter term priorities to point you in the direction of where you want to go for the next couple of months. But having priorities is not enough – many managers, who know where they want to go, find it hard to get into their priorities because they lack the energy to get started, and that comes from making priorities into tasks.

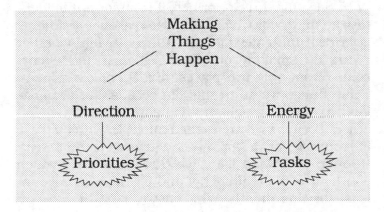

Getting Direction and Focus

Setting priorities for yourself is a straightforward exercise. Take five to ten minutes to draw up a list of all the things you would like to achieve or get done in the next few

months – it could be a month or six months depending on your preferred time horizon. Apart from considering the things you have to get done, also identify the things you want to get done. What do you want to achieve, take on as a challenge or simply give more of your time to in the next couple of months? In five minutes most managers come up with at least ten things on which they want to make progress in the near future.

However, while it is easy to draw up a wish list, we really only have energy for two or three as priorities at any one time. Focus is the key to effectiveness in most walks of life and lack of focus one of the ways in which managers give away their influence and ability to achieve things. The "Golden Rule of Three", which applies to many situations, offers a simple guide in setting priorities suggesting that more than three is too many – by focusing on too many things you often end up focusing on nothing.

In selecting three priorities, it is important to identify the things for which you have real energy. Energy is critical to achieving most things in life, whether giving up smoking or passing exams, and energy comes from only two places, anxiety or excitement. Some things we do in this life because we are anxious, about our weight or an important deadline, and others because we are excited about learning a piece of software or a foreign language. As you scan through your wish list, pick three things for which you have some real energy and let the others go, at least for this month. Who knows, next month you may have more energy for other things.

As newly elected president of his local tennis club, John was keen to give direction and make some progress in the short-term. From a list of challenges for the next year the committee agreed on three as priorities over the next three months.

1) To redecorate the premises.
2) To upgrade the bar food menu.
3) To attract a higher percentage of members on a regular basis.

While not losing sight of the need to run a good tennis programme for the year, a limited number of priorities for action gave the committee, and the members, a sense of where the club was going and John a clear brief to succeed as president.

Make Energy for Priorities

While they may look invitingly simple, trying to make progress on long-term priorities is like eating an elephant, hard to start, difficult to digest and, once started, hard to finish. Yet the analogy does suggest some practical disciplines for managing priorities.

RULES FOR EATING ELEPHANTS

Rule 1   Make them into a clear challenge.

Rule 2   Break them into bits.

Rule 3   Start wherever the elephant will let you.

Rule 4   Keep your eye on the elephants while you are fighting off the ants.

Many long-term priorities are vague and aspirational, with a familiar ring that suggests they have been around for a while. Like aspirations to give up smoking or lose weight, the energy for most priorities does not last long.

It helps to energise the bigger and more difficult things if you firstly make them into clear challenges. Rather than committing to "get fit" in the next couple of months set yourself the target of running a 10k mini-marathon in May, losing 10lbs by 30 June or joining a gym and exercising twice a week for the next two months. If you want to improve teamwork in your area or implement a new distribution system – start by making it into a specific demand – identify what you want to achieve or what will be in place when you are finished. Making priorities into a clear challenge is similar to going for the bullseye rather than aiming for the target – if you miss the bullseye at least you hit the target, while if you aim for the target and miss, you hit nothing.

> Improve Teamwork
> in my area.
>
> $\lessgtr$
>
> Appoint and train three
> team leaders by
> 31 March.

> Implement a new
> Distribution System
>
> $\lessgtr$
>
> Reach the 24-hour
> delivery promise to at
> least 90 per cent of
> customers by 31 May.

Start on the Easy Bits

Although making priorities into challenges helps to make them more accessible, they are still difficult to achieve because the energy, for most managers, is in what needs to be done for today rather than what they want to get done in

> **WORD TO THE WISE**
> You eat elephants by breaking them into bits and starting on the easy bits.

the next two months. Ask yourself this: "When do people get real energy for exams, projects, reports, summer holidays or Christmas?" Correct – about a week or ten days before the event or the deadline. Things that are two or three months down the road are often subject to procrastination or are left undone until the urgency of a deadline ensures that they are done stressfully enough, they won't be taken on as priorities in the future.

The way to make energy for the bigger things in the job is to look at what you could do in the next week or two to get some quick and easy success. If one of your priorities over the next couple of months is to "appoint and train three new team leaders" consider all the short-term tasks you could do in the next week to eat the first piece of the elephant: do up a job description, put an advertisement on the staff notice board or agree a pay structure with your boss. When you have considered all the short-term options, use the golden rule of three to pick a few things you will absolutely commit to achieving this week.

Figure 4.2: Break Priorities Into Bits

Take one of your priorities for the next couple of months and brainstorm all the things you could do in the next week to get started. Think of simple things, such as telephoning some-one, having a meeting, reading a book, doing a one page outline or planning a visit. And do not put sequence into the tasks which kills energy if you find your progress blocked by one step in the sequence.

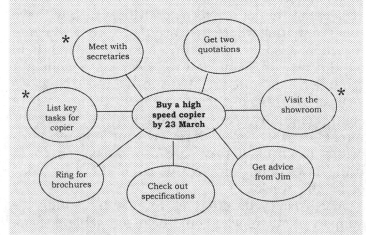

Now, asterisk the three things you will commit to doing this week, preferably tasks that are accessible because they are cheap, easy or exciting. More important than doing the right things first is doing something that will give you an early success.

Not only is it easier to schedule time for short-term tasks than for priorities but they also fit the time-frame that is available to most managers. Breaking elephants into bits and starting on the easy bits also guarantees some success in the short-term and success breeds energy to keep going on the bigger things. If, by the end of the first week, you have completed the three things to which you committed you will have more energy for the next chunk of the elephant – committing to another three things for next week.

Keep the Important Things Up Front

In the normal course of events, it is very easy to lose sight of the bigger things to the overwhelming volume of short-term demands on your time. As a way of keeping the longer term priorities in view, have them in writing where they are visible commitments to action. Also, keep them up front by having them on the wall in front of your desk as a constant reminder that you are there to achieve things as well as do things – on longer term things "out of sight" generally means "out of mind". At the beginning of each day or week review your long-term priorities to check if there are any tasks you could bring down onto your weekly plan or diary for today or for this week.

Also, keep your priorities in view by getting the support of others who could help you achieve them, such as your boss or key staff. Most big challenges in life, (e.g. losing weight, writing a book or finishing a thesis) need the support of others to keep going, or at least not to block your efforts. Keep repeating your priorities as a way of renewing your commitment to them – the best way to give up smoking or lose weight is to keep telling people you are doing it and get them to gently but firmly nag you into action.

Track What you Want to Control

One of the reasons for making elephants into concrete challenges and breaking them into bits is it makes them easier to track and control. If one of your priorities is to lose 10 lbs by 30 June, a few tasks that could help you to get some immediate progress include drawing up a weight loss chart, buying a pair of bathroom scales or weighing yourself today.

Tracking things is often enough to make them happen. When a group of new home owners were asked to take part in an experiment on conserving domestic energy, some were given a very challenging target of reducing their electricity consumption by 20 per cent, some an easy target of 2 per cent and others were assigned to a control group who were given no target. All three groups were given daily feedback by the researchers updating a graph attached to the patio windows. The results of the experiment showed that those who were set a challenging target did the best, but equally interesting, those in the control group who were just given feedback also significantly reduced their energy consumption.

Simple methods for tracking priorities include setting a target for the number of hours a week you intend to give to a project and recording each hour or half hour as you complete it – many things get done if you simply give them time. Alternatively, if you want to reduce material wastage or improve customer service in your area, agree a standard and share feedback on it each week with your staff – better still, get your staff to record and report the data themselves. If you want to improve one of your personal habits, start recording the number of cigarettes, pieces of chocolate, fruit, or hours of sleep you get each day. As a way of tracking progress on projects, set a deadline for completion and break them into mini-deadlines for each stage. If you fail to meet one of the mini-deadlines brainstorm a list of things you could do to get back on track and select three as commitments for next week.

When Jan Carlson took over as President of SAS it was in serious trouble, with losses in excess of $17 million. He soon found that he was heading a company that had drifted into many things such as charters, holidays and freight and was doing none of them very well. Setting out to re-establish SAS as Europe's premier business airline, Carlson identified punctuality as the number one priority. As a way of monitoring progress, Carlson had a viewing screen installed in his office with details of all flight delays. If there was a problem he would personally ring the airport, sometimes talking directly to the flight crew to resolve the issue or to compliment them when they got things right. In one short year SAS became the top on-time airline in Europe.

Review your Progress Frequently

The process of breaking priorities into chunks also makes them easier to manage on a daily basis – it is much easier to schedule tasks into your day than to make progress on priorities. Check your priorities frequently and as you get the tasks done acknowledge their completion by ticking them off the list, then identify others as commitments. Also bring new tasks on board as other possibilities come to mind. When you have completed the initial tasks on "getting fit", look for more creative and adventurous tasks, such as getting details of a health farm, joining Weight Watchers or ringing a couple of friends who may be interested in forming a walking group.

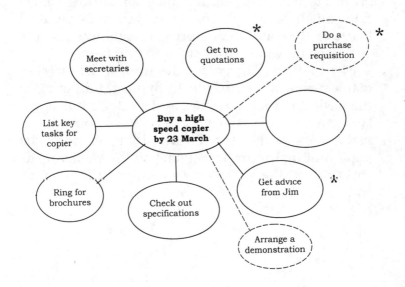

Finally, as a simple discipline for ensuring that you renew your priorities on a regular basis make a note in your diary one day each month to draw up a new wish list and select three more priorities. Not only will it give you a sense of moving towards your longer term ambitions, but there is also a buzz from sitting down once a month and doing up a new list. While some of your priorities may extend over a few months (for example, writing this book has been a priority for me over the past eight months) others will reach completion and can be replaced with fresh priorities as new challenges become more focal.

Managers are inclined to take their priorities for granted, hoping in some way they will get time and energy for the bigger and more strategic things in the job. However, while they may be convinced of the need to make things happen as well as do things for today, the evidence is that managers give very little time to what they say is important for the future. Not only are long-term priorities less focal on a day to day basis, but most of the big things take much longer to complete than was planned because they are often started reluctantly and the enthusiasm wanes early on in the process.

The only way to reverse the trap, which sees so many managers overwhelmed by operating work to the neglect of their proactive and strategic functions, is to start finding energy for the things you want to make happen for the future. Hanging onto the important tasks means focusing on the elephants as you fight off the ants that can so easily undermine your time and efforts as a manager.

REMEMBER

DO:

- Make time to be proactive by having, and working to, long-term priorities.

- Remember the golden rule of three: more then three priorities is too many.

- Work to the priorities by breaking them into short-term tasks.

- Find a way to keep priorities up front and track them as a way of controlling them.

- Review your short-term tasks frequently and reset your priorities monthly.

DO NOT:

- Let the reactive side of your job overwhelm the proactive side.

Chapter 5

Schedule For The Important Things

This chapter will help you to:

- understand why routine and urgency drive out importance in the job;

- recognise the need to schedule time for the important things;

- start using a 'to do' list, weekly planner and diary to schedule for importance.

Schedule For The Important Things

In the typical working day many things get done because they are familiar routines, e.g. opening the post, checking e-mails or responding to post-it notes. Not only do they offer managers the opportunity of an easy reward but they are

also part of the buzz in the job. Other things for which managers have little difficulty committing their time include institutionalised activities, e.g. meetings, visits or appointments, which are easily scheduled into their day and are seldom questioned.

Some things are also done because they offer attractive opportunities even when managers are weighed down with work and over commitment. Imagine your boss telling you that he wanted someone to represent the company on a 10-day all-expenses paid trade mission to Thailand. While recognising that you are the obvious person to go, he is also aware of your work pressure and suggests that you take an hour or two to think about it. Well, do you think you can make the ten days? Probably, if you are like other managers who have been posed the same question. How do you do it? Easy. You take your diary and a pen and draw a line through the ten days and over the top write one word: Thailand.

Ask any manager for his major continuing problem and he will normally reply "time". Time to think, time to plan, time to talk with my people. Yet the same man finds the time for food and for sleep, for Sundays and for holidays. But these are institutionalised priorities – time for the future is not.

Understanding Organisations
Charles Handy

But, unlike institutionalised activities, or an attractive overseas conference, managers find it much more difficult to get time for their longer term challenges, like developing teamwork, improving communications or completing projects. Those kind of things do not get done unless they are scheduled into the manager's day, week or month.

TIME FOR IMPORTANCE

Managing time is all about making choices, many of which are dictated by urgency, which not only tends to take precedence over importance but often drives out the important things especially where those tasks are important but not urgent.

I met a client for lunch the other day. He had arranged the meeting to discuss management development needs in his area. As we sat down to lunch his mobile phone rang and, from the conversation, I gathered it was a minor technical problem. As telephone reception was poor in the dining room he excused himself to continue his conversation in the lobby and after a few minutes I decided to go ahead and eat. Twenty five minutes later, when he returned, I had finished my lunch, his was cold, and very soon afterwards he had to excuse himself to get to another appointment. We never did get to discuss the issue of developing his people. Interestingly enough, a couple of weeks earlier his boss had described him as an "operational manager".

Both urgency and importance have to be managed into the day – the trick is not letting urgency become the driving force for your work load. As well as making appropriate responses to the routine demands you also need to get mileage out of your day by finding time for the longer term issues. Scheduling your time effectively means pushing the barriers of importance so that you end up doing the things that have to be done but also making time to achieve the things you want to get done.

	2	3
Urgent ↑	• Minor Crisis • Routine Problems • Interruptions • Ad Hoc Meetings	• Deadlines • Daily Key Tasks • Major Problems • Crisis or Blockages
	1	4
	• Routine Correspondence • Many Phone Calls • Time Wasters • Trivia	• Long-term Tasks • Projects • Developing Staff • Future Planning

Important ⟶

Box 1: Unimportant and Non-urgent Tasks

You should be trying to let some things in the day go either by not doing them at all or giving them less of your time. Less urgent or routine things, such as paperwork or handling queries, could be given to others – let someone else open the post or attend that routine meeting. Also, consider doing the less important things at times of the day when you have least energy or less time.

Box 2: Urgent but Unimportant Tasks

Urgent but less important things, such as minor crises or routine problems, can be dealt with by giving them sparing amounts of time or scheduling them for later in the day. Routinely urgent issues could also be handled by developing procedures or training others to deal with them.

Box 3: Urgent and Important Tasks

Some things are urgent and important because there is a crisis or a deadline, or because your priorities shift, e.g. a key customer needs material urgently to complete a rush order or a machine has gone down and a decision has to be made to get it back in production. In that event, the daily schedule may have to be rearranged to respond immediately to that task or to do the most urgent piece now and deal with the rest later.

Box 4: Important but Non-urgent Tasks

Other things are important but are not driven by urgency. Many of the functions so critical to long-term effectiveness, such as planning, reviewing progress on projects, developing new systems, or improving quality and service, are not driven by routine or urgency but by managers giving them time. Proactive work that has no immediate urgency is in danger of being deferred unless it is diarised or identified as a priority and broken into chunks that can be managed on a daily or a weekly basis.

While the tasks in boxes 1 and 2 need to be organised effectively into your day the tasks in boxes 3 and 4 need to be scheduled to make them happen. Simple ways of scheduling time for the important things in your day, week and month include the use a 'to do' list, a weekly planner or a diary.

	Do it later	Do it now
	Delegate	Do part
Urgent ↑	Develop staff	Delegate part
	Drop	Diary
	Defer	Decimate
	Delegate	Deadline

Important ⟶

CARPE DIEM: SEIZE THE DAY

One of the most common work habits is keeping lists of things you are trying to get done in the day. The main problem with lists, apart from the fact that they get longer and longer, is that most people start on the easy things first: the logic being, "I'll get rid of the easy things and then I'll get into the bigger ones". Of course it does not work that way – usually we find more and more easy things to prevent us from getting into the important things, which are often relegated to the back end of the afternoon or transferred to yet another list for tomorrow.

> My mother was an inveterate list maker throughout her 90 years. We grew to dread helping her when we came back to stay at the farm, as her list contained such items as: paint barn, fence farm, plant lower field, bring in harvest. One morning as I sat watching her finish her daily list, she smiled with satisfaction and crossed off the first item. "Mother," I said, "how could you have already accomplished something?" Then I looked over her shoulder. She had crossed out the first two words: 'Make list'.
>
> Opel Nestingen

One simple way to ensure that you balance urgency and importance in your day is to keep a 'to do' list. While it starts life as a simple list, what makes it into a management tool is that you prioritise the activities as *As*, *Bs*, *Cs* and *Ds* and work to those priorities. The *As* are tasks that you must get done today and there are never more than three. The *Bs* are things you should get done today – the *As* in waiting that may become priorities but only when you get the *As* done. *Cs* are things you want to put on the list so you do not forget them and *Ds* are things you want to give to others to do.

One of the most quoted stories on time management concerns Charles Scwab, former President of Bethlehem Steel and his efficiency expert Ivy Lee. When Scwab asked for some advice on how to speed up his work flow, Lee promised that in 20 minutes he could improve his efficiency by 50 per cent. Handing him a piece of paper he told him to write down his six most important tasks for tomorrow and to number them in order of importance. He suggested that Scwab start on item 1 first thing in the morning and work on it until it was finished and then go onto item 2 and not to be too concerned about how many things he completed in the day, since he would always be working on the most important things first. He advised Scwab to persist until he was convinced of its usefulness and to have his men try it too and to send him a cheque for what the idea was worth. A few weeks later Lee received a cheque for $25,000 as payment for the most profitable lesson Scwab had ever learned as a manager.

The secret of working with a 'to do' list is to start as early as possible on the *As*, for two reasons. Firstly, most people have their peak energy early in the day, between 8.00 am and 11.00 am, so hitting the *As* early means you are working on the most important things at times of the day when you have your best mental energy. Conversely it also means you are working on the less important things at times of the day when you have least mental energy.

WORD TO THE WISE
By continuing to focus on the important tasks you will always be doing the first things first.

A second reason for starting early on the *As* is that success is the best way of creating energy for the rest of the day. When you have completed the three *As*, simply reprioritise some of the *Bs* into *As* – in that way you are always doing the first things first.

USING A TO 'DO LIST'

- Review or redo your 'to do' list first thing in the morning.

- Check your long-term priorities and bring tasks down onto the list.

- Prioritise the tasks as *As*, *Bs*, *Cs* and *Ds*.

- Start early on the *As*.

- Re-prioritise your activities as you go through the day.

- Keep the list on your desk as a reminder to do the first things first.

Tips on To Do Lists

Keep the main thing as the main thing at all times. One of the most common frustrations shared by managers is of not getting enough mileage out of their efforts in the day. Get a head start on the day by deciding where you want to go with it and by focusing your attention on the main things first. Get the pleasure of crossing *As* off the list as you complete them, and at the end of the day it is easy to see whether it was a productive or a busy day: Did you get the *As* done or was it mainly *Cs* and *Bs* you completed? While starting on the *As* is no guarantee that you will get everything done in the day, tackling them first means that you are always focusing on the most important things.

Eat the elephants in chunks. As you do up your 'to do' list each morning make sure that it reflects what you want to get done for the long-term as well as for today. If you have broken your major priorities into tasks, see if you can draw any of them down onto your 'to do' list for today. If some tasks are too big to do as daily tasks then break them into smaller pieces that can be done in a half hour or an hour in the day.

To Do List:

B	Invoice Kintech Ltd
A	Write IDB Proposal
D	Photocopy Meeting Notes
B	Check C.S. Progress
B	Book Flight London
C	Ring Jim Magee

Use the golden rule of three. One of the biggest temptations with 'to do' lists is making more than three things into *As* on the basis that everything is important. But the problem with making five or six things into *As* is that you are rapidly getting back to a simple list again and you still have to make a choice about which tasks to do first. Discipline yourself to having no more than three *As* on your list at any one time, and even if you complete them by 9.30 am, simply re-prioritise some of the *Bs* into *As*. Tasks which are *Bs* this morning may well become *As* this afternoon and items which are *Cs* today may well become *As* tomorrow.

Plan the work and work the plan. While a 'to do' list gives you a sense of where you want to go with today, it is not a timetable for the day – the beauty is that it gives you both focus and flexibility. Should something urgent or important arise during the day you may have to add it to your list as an *A*, and if during the day there is a crisis you may have to forget the list for a while, but always with the intention of getting back to it as soon as possible. The fact that you cannot plan everything does not mean you should not plan.

THANK GOODNESS FOR MONDAYS

It is all too easy to get to Friday with that uncomfortable feeling it was a hell off a week but you have little to show for all your efforts. Like the cowboy who jumped onto his horse and rode off in all directions the danger for managers is giving away your energy by trying to go in too many directions at once. One way of avoiding the dangerous drift into 'busyness' is to get a clear sense of direction at the beginning of the week, to monitor your progress through the five days and, on Friday, to review your success as a way of planning for the next week.

Allow yourself ten minutes on a Monday morning to reflect on what you want to get done with your week. List all the jobs you need to get done in the next five days and select three of them as priorities. Break them into smaller tasks, such as writing something, telephoning someone, reading something or meeting someone, and prioritise each task, with no more than three as *As*. Start into the As on Monday and as you go through the week reprioritise the list, making the *Bs* and *Cs* into *As*. At the end of the week review what kind of week it was: was it efficient in the sense that you got a lot of the routine things done or were you effective in getting the important things completed?

WEEKLY PLANNER

1. Prepare for CP Presentation	Plan Outline	A
	Prepare Outline	D
	Do a Rehearsal	B
	Arrange Notes	C
2. Do 2 Staff Appraisals	Review Goals	B
	Arrange Meetings	A
	Fill in Forms	C

USING A WEEKLY PLANNER

- On Monday morning list the main things you want to get done this week.
- Identify three as priorities for the week. Break those into tasks and prioritise them as *A, B, C* or *D*.
- Start early on the *As* and as you complete them reprioritise the *Bs* into *As*.
- Review your progress daily and review the week on Friday.

Tips for Managing a Weekly Planner

Combine your weekly and daily plans. The place to have a weekly planner is on the wall in front of your desk as a reminder of the challenges and your progress in the week. As you complete each task cross it off the list and reprioritise the rest. Alternatively, you could draw tasks down from your weekly planner onto a 'to do' list and prioritise them as daily activities. A weekly planner also combines nicely with a diary by blocking out specific times in the week when you intend to do certain tasks.

As MD of a computer services company, Detta has a one hour meeting with her management team every Monday morning from 9.00-10.00 am. In that hour they each report what was achieved in the previous week and how it relates to their long-term priorities. They also use the time to share their priorities for this week. At that meeting, they have an opportunity to ask their colleagues for support in advance of looking for assistance – as a result there are no surprises and most important issues can be left until the next Monday meeting.

Share the weekly challenges with others. It can help remind your staff what you are trying to get done with your week if you share your priorities as a way of getting their support. If there are tasks on your weekly planner that you want to delegate to others, do it early in the week and if you delegate your *Ds* on a Monday put a reminder in your diary to monitor progress on them sometime in the middle of the week – do not leave checking whether things have been done until Friday.

MAKE APPOINTMENTS TO YOURSELF

Most people use a diary as an *aide memoir*, in case they forget dates or their commitments to others. Managers also get some comfort from having a full diary, which conveniently lets them off the hook with having to plan their day or week – all they have to do is follow the diary. The main problem is that many things we commit to diaries should probably not have been agreed at all, and many things that are put in diaries are for the benefit of others rather than commitments to our own priorities.

USING A DIARY

- At the beginning of each week block out time for tasks such as planning or project work.
- Review the monthly priorities frequently and schedule time for them in your diary.
- Record deadlines on delegated tasks and monitoring dates along the way.
- Record trigger dates to review and reset your monthly priorities.
- Set deadlines and mini-deadlines on projects and use your diary to monitor them.

One way to start making more effective use of your diary, is to block out chunks of time for the things you want to get done and not letting anything get in the way of those commitments. Also, build some breathing space into potentially time-consuming commitments to others by promising to come back in a day or two to confirm them. Stop taking your diary into meetings, if you tend to make commitments that you later regret and always ask yourself if there is an easier way of doing things that would take less of your time (e.g. exchanging a couple of e-mails or having a phone conversation) rather than agreeing to a meeting or writing a report.

TIPS ON USING A DIARY

Make time to think. Start using your diary to block out time for thinking or long-term planning, neither of which need to be solitary reflections. Schedule an hour this week to scan a few journal articles, write up an outline plan for the next three months or have a free wheeling meeting with a couple of colleagues.

> Most people think only once or twice a year. I have made an international reputation for myself by thinking once or twice a week.
>
> George Bernard Shaw

Chunk your diary commitments. The weekly planner or 'to do' list can be combined with a diary by blocking out specific hours in your day or week to get certain tasks done, such as finishing a report, drafting a letter or planning a presentation. Alternatively, plan to spend an hour on a big task as a way of getting some initial success and energy for what might otherwise be an overwhelming job. Committing an hour to planning a difficult assignment is often enough to begin to see it more clearly and as being more manageable.

If a big task is likely to take four or five hours to complete then make it easier for yourself by breaking it into hourly chunks and scheduling an hour on five separate days. Most authors break the long and solitary task of writing a book into chunks by committing a couple of hours to writing each day, or writing a certain number of words a day. I personally use a stopwatch to work an hour at a time on my bigger tasks and, at the end of an hour, I reward myself with a 15-minute break.

Schedule important tasks for the mornings. One of the most interesting pieces of data emerging from time log analysis is how many routine activities are scheduled into the mornings when managers have their best mental energy. Make it a rule to schedule your most important tasks into the mornings and the less demanding things into the afternoons when you have least mental energy. Most routine meetings are better held in the afternoons, as would most travel, routine correspondence, managing by wandering around, responding to telephone messages or answering queries.

Commit time to yourself. One of the major stress factors in managing is the feeling that other people and events are controlling your time. Yet many managers who complain about being out of control with their time also let others decide their appointments or determine the length of their meetings and telephone calls. In an effort to reclaim his time, Robert Townsend, then President of Avis, decided to sack his secretary and to answer his own phone. He claimed that it allowed him to decide when to call people back or to plan when he would be available for interruptions – at all other times he instructed the receptionist to take full messages and let people know when he would reply. It sounds dramatic, but if you need more time for planning and thinking, or simply for doing the things you want to get done with your day, then make sure you do not leave yourself at the mercy of others.

Plan to relax. As a way of avoiding the over commitment that often leads to stress, schedule some time in your diary for exercise or relaxation before you start making commitments to others. Decide early in the year when you are going to take your holidays and schedule a few short breaks in the year and make them solid commitments to yourself. Schedule personal time for exercise, for your family or for networking and where possible make them regular commitments so they become a routine part of your weekly or monthly schedule (e.g. every

Thursday evening for the gym or a family event on the first Monday of every month).

> Over the years I've had many executives come to me and say with pride, "Boy, last year I worked so hard that I didn't take any vacation." It's actually nothing to be proud of. I always feel like responding, "You dummy. You mean to tell me that you can take responsibility for an $80 million project and you can't plan two weeks out of the year to go off with your family and have some fun?"
>
> Lee Iaccocca

As a manager, it is all too easy to end up being organised around the wrong things, spending most of your time fighting fires. Apart from making time for the routine and operational parts of the job, you also need to make time for the things you really want to get done as a manager by scheduling time for them. Scheduling time for the real challenges in the job is also the best way of ensuring that you give less time to the things you should be letting go.

Making time to do what is important in your day, week and month is critical for taking your major responsibilities beyond aspiration to reality. If you say that something is a priority, and you are not giving it hours in your day or week then, in reality, it is not a priority. Working to key tasks and priorities is simply a function of paying attention to them by giving them your time – some things get done because they are familiar routines and other things you need to make happen.

REMEMBER

DO:

- Make time for important tasks in the day and week by prioritising them and working to the priorities.

- Use your diary as a tool in making time for important tasks rather than simply for recording commitments to others.

- Complete important tasks in your peak energy hours.

DO NOT:

- Let routine and urgency get in the way of the important tasks.

Chapter 6

Delegate Routine And Responsibility

This chapter will help you to:

- clarify the difference between delegating work and responsibility;

- schedule time in your day and week for delegating and empowering your staff;

- manage reverse delegation by pushing the monkeys back to your staff.

Delegate Routine And Responsibility

Why is it that so many managers are driven by routine and urgency rather than by the important tasks in their job? Why is it that many managers see themselves as responsible for everything and so many of their staff see themselves as responsible for nothing? Why are so many managers stretched and overworked while their staff feel under-utilised and bored? Why do so many managers end up doing what they should patently be getting other people to do?

One of the main excuses used by managers for doing things that they should be giving to others is that it is easier to do it themselves. However, the problem with doing things yourself is that others never learn to do them and over time come to regard them as part of your job. Lack of trained staff is another excuse offered by managers for doing the work of others: "I can't give it to Jack, he is really busy." Managers rarely challenge how busy their subordinates are – in my experience most people end up being busy, but busy doing what?

However, the most common reason for managers continuing to hang on to what they should be giving away to others has little to do with their staff. Managers continue to hang on to much of the routine in the job because it is familiar territory and the human condition is that we do not let go of familiar things easily. How many of you have still got cupboards or attics full of old schoolbooks, clothes or letters you should have got rid of years ago? How many people stay in dead-end jobs or hang on to bad relationships because it is difficult to let go?

You spent your life sitting on brambles and wouldn't get up in case someone took your place.
Hugh Leonard

Letting go of familiar routines in life is essentially a function of having other things on which to focus. One example is the Olympic athletes who, in the lead up to the Olympic Games, give up many things in their lives, such as their eating habits, certain foods, their social lives, savings and even their jobs. They let go with certainty because they have their sights clearly set on qualifying for the Games, improving their personal best, representing their country or winning a medal. Likewise, in the absence of clear goals and priorities, it is difficult to let go of the comfort of daily routine and urgency, much of which in theory is the work of your staff.

Apart from finding it easier to delegate if you have clear challenges in your own job, it also helps if you treat delegation as a broad process for letting go. There are in fact four places you can let go of things.

1. By giving more responsibility to your staff.
2. By saying "no" more often to those who dump on you from above without appreciating your priorities.
3. By pushing things back to colleagues who may have found you a convenient place to dump their problems.
4. By using the waste paper basket as a tool in delegation. The "law of calculated neglect" reminds us that many things if left alone will simply go away.

Figure 6.1: Letting Go

Draw up a list of the things you would like to let go of in your job. For each activity estimate the amount of time you currently spend and the amount by which you would like to reduce that commitment. Use the four strategies in delegation as a guide to identifying how many hours you could let go each week. Pick one as a priority for the next month and find ways to track your success.

Task	Current Hours	Proposed Hours	Saving	Methods
Routine Meetings	8	5	3	• Delegate to Jim • Reduce own meetings by 1/2 hour
Travelling	12	6	6	• Meet managers half way • Take the train

Letting Go of Responsibility

While managers generally recognise the need to say "no" more often to others, or to push back problems to their colleagues, one of the main obstacles to letting go is getting key staff to share their responsibilities. Many of the important things you are trying to get done as a manager require the commitment of your staff, not just a willing pair of hands. If, for example, you ask one of your staff to photocopy some notes for a conference at best you are delegating work because the task is clear and unambiguous, you can see them doing it or at least can check the results. If, on the other hand, you ask them to take responsibility for the administrative workload at the conference, you are letting go of a broader task where the person has discretion in how they do it and you cannot control their input as easily. The essential difference between delegating work and responsibility is that letting go of responsibility also means you have to trust people.

Did you hear the story of the climber who fell off a cliff face and managed to save himself by grabbing a small shrub growing from the rock. Suspended in mid air, he yells out, "Is there anybody up there."

After a couple of seconds a voice booms back, "Yes, I am here."

"Who is it?" shouts the climber.

"It is God," booms back the voice,"I will save you."

"What shall I do?" asks the climber.

Back comes the voice,"Let go of the branch and I will catch you."

A minute goes by before the anxious voice starts up again,"Is there any one else up there?"

Letting go does not mean blind trust, if things go wrong it is still your responsibility as well as theirs. Yet managers do have to learn to trust their staff with real responsibility and the only way to do this is by giving it time. Although, as a manager, you may believe that you already spend enough time with your staff, most of those daily contacts are on minor issues or problems. Getting to the point where you can trust your staff with almost the same degree of responsibility as yourself requires 'quality time', to clarify what you want from them, to get them to take ownership for the task and to encourage and recognise them for sharing the responsibility. As with personal relationships, you do not trust people unless you spend time developing and sustaining the relationship in four important ways.

1. Tell your Staff What you Want

Over 70 per cent of employees in a recent survey were unclear about what their boss wanted from them or how their job performance would be measured. Not only are managers unclear about what they want from their staff, but they also have a habit of expressing their demands in vague language, e.g. "I want you to deal with","handle","liaise" or "co-ordinate." Managers also give mixed messages to their staff, e.g. "I want you to take full responsibility, but let me know if there are problems" or "Do it your way but get my input." And when questioned if they are clear about what they are being asked to do most staff give a non-committal response, e.g. "Yes, I think so."

> **WORD TO THE WISE**
> The difference between delegating work and delegating responsibility is 'trust'.

Apart from being unclear about what they want from their staff, managers also believe that saying things once is enough. Even young children learn that if you want something you have to ask more than once – the first time you ask for an ice cream or a bar of chocolate you have not even been heard. Similarly, it is not enough to tell your staff once what you want from them, you have to find a variety of ways of reminding them so they hear the message clearly above all the other demands in the job.

One of the best ways to remind your staff of their responsibilities is to agree goals with them. A simple process involves sitting down individually or as a group and talking about the challenges in their job for the next two to three months. Out of that discussion get them to identify three things as priorities and identify tasks that could help them eat the first part of the elephant. Keep a copy of their goals and encourage their progress by asking periodically how they are doing. At the end of each month have a short review meeting as a way of rewarding their progress and coach them on finding additional tasks to fuel the next part of the journey.

Figure 6.2: Agree Goals with Staff

John agreed two goals with Mary at her 3-monthly job review. To relieve him of some of the administrative work in the training function, he wanted her to take on the purchasing of all training course materials, while Mary identified a need to develop her skills at computer graphics. Agreeing both of them as goals, John helped Mary to identify tasks for the next month that would help her get progress in both areas.

Goals - 3 months	Tasks - 1 Month
Take on ordering of all stationery supplies by 30 June	Meet with two suppliers
	Draw up stock sheet
	Price articles in stock
	Get catalogue from suppliers
Get certificate in computer graphics by 28 August	Install software on PC
	Book three lessons
	Two hours a week coaching

As the month went by, Mary tackled simple tasks that she could schedule into her week and John was able to give her encouragement and reward as he saw her making progress. At the end of the month, they sat down for fifteen minutes to review the task list and talk about what she intended to do for the next month.

2. Get Ownership and Commitment

One of the most frustrating aspects of giving responsibility to others is the feeling that they are not fully committed to the task. Real ownership for delegation is different than head nodding – ownership is something that is taken and cannot be assumed. Ownership is also rejected in many subtle ways when staff feel they are being dumped on or find their boss taking back responsibility by interfering in the detail.

As a manager, you need to make time to coach your staff so they keep ownership, but you also need to resist the temptation to tell them how to do it, otherwise the task still remains your responsibility – if things go wrong it was your decision to do it that way. On the other hand giving broad responsibility to someone without supporting them is dumping and when people feel dumped on they have many ways to get back at you.

Coaching is a process for helping people commit to the task and getting them excited about the journey. Professional coaches rarely tell their charges what to do, instead they inspire them, using two basic skills. They "listen", to get them talking and to encourage them to think things through for themselves, "Where do you see yourself in the next three months?","How would you tackle the problem?","What are your options on this?","Where would you like to start?","What's a first step?"). The other skill that coaches use is "feedback" – giving the person positive encouragement or correction by presenting them with their picture e.g. "I feel really good about your progress", "Your sales are 20 per cent above target", "I had three more complaints about service in your area last week".

In a study carried out on communications in a public utility, 76 per cent of the foremen reported always getting ideas from their staff on job problems, however, only 16 per cent of subordinates reported being so consulted by their bosses.

Tell your people what you want and coach them on how to do it. Get the pleasure of seeing them take control and being available if they need help.

3. Monitor What you Give Away

You never completely let go of responsibility, you share it – if something goes wrong, it is still your neck on the line. For your sake, and for the benefit of your staff, you need to follow up what you give away but make sure that you do not undermine your staff's confidence. There are a number of unobtrusive ways to monitor delegation.

- **MBWA (managing by wandering around):** commit time in your diary or 'to do' list to make casual contacts with staff to find out how things are going.

- **Naive listening**: rather than asking about the detail of a task, use open ended questions, such as "Where are you at?", "How is it going?", "What obstacles are you meeting?"

- **Group reviews**: get your team to review progress on their goals in public where they can get affirmation and feedback from the group. In that way they are being challenged by their peers rather than by the boss.

- **Regular one on ones**: have frequent 'off the job' chats with your staff and schedule time for them. At those meetings, which need only to be ten or fifteen minutes a month, keep the balance between listening and talking to about 70 per cent to 30 per cent. Give your staff a real chance to hear themselves and always have something in store to reward them.

Jim decided to involve his staff in the planning process for a major sales conference. As a group they had several planning meetings and everyone knew their responsibilities for the three days. But on the first day of the conference, Jim's style changed. Instead of leaving his staff to do their jobs, he began to interfere in the smallest detail, pulling them up on minor issues, grabbing things back from people if there was the slightest of problem and harassing them to do things the way he wanted them done. By the end of the first day, his staff were beginning to lose their motivation and confidence and Jim was becoming increasingly involved in the detail as he saw a lack of responsibility in his staff.

4. Reward and Recognise their Progress

Like most challenges in life, people take on responsibility for the recognition of others. Although your staff may not volunteer to take on extra work, even for more money, they will often do things for someone they respect.

In psychology, the simple *law of effect* says a lot about motivating staff in stating "things which are rewarded tend to be repeated and things which are unrewarded tend to be extinguished". In encouraging children to take responsibility for their learning, parents have no problem using a great deal of recognition and praise to encourage their efforts. While the effect of praise and encouragement on children is clear, most managers still undervalue the power of recognition on their staff, finding it much easier to criticise them for what they do not achieve than to praise them for what they do right.

Figure 6.3: Reward and Recognition

Yes / No

- Do you sufficiently reward and encourage your staff?
- Do you tend to punish the poor performers?
- Do your people know what they have to do to get rewarded?
- Are you rewarding the right things?
- Are there some things you need to start rewarding?
- Could you find more creative ways to reward your people?
- Do you know how your staff feel about the recognition they get?

Though some managers intuitively know how to get the best out of their people, for most it means scheduling time to reward and recognise the behaviours you want to encourage. Apart from recognising the good performers, who often know they are doing well, it is important to find ways to encourage the poor performers by praising them for what they do approximately right rather than waiting for them to do things exactly right.

Identify two things you could do to improve reward and recognition in your area (do not plan to do more than two things otherwise it will appear that you have read a book). Schedule those activities into your diary as solid commitments and make time for them in the next month.

- Have monthly one on ones.

- Celebrate project completion or meeting targets.

- Spend more time with poor performers.

- Have occasional off-site meetings to share views.

- Have an ideas or suggestion scheme.

- Draw up a training plan.

- Celebrate birthdays or anniversaries.

- Do more MBWA.

- Regularise team briefings to tell staff how things are going.

- Have team meetings at which staff report progress on their goals.

- Reward one piece of good work a day.

- Send thank you notes for jobs well done.

- Set up task groups and get staff to chair them.

- Give one piece of encouragement each day.

- Get more details of staff – children, hobbies, commitments, etc.

EMPOWERING YOUR STAFF TO EXCEL

The control function, which was traditionally exercised by middle managers, has given way in most organisations to more participative approaches aimed at encouraging shared responsibility for broader issues, such as quality, service and innovation. Developing a participative culture that pushes responsibility down to lower levels, also means that managers have to adopt styles of supervision that empower their staff to see beyond the narrow job description. Empowerment means identifying the future challenges in the area and inviting staff to share those challenges by raising their expectations of themselves.

> Teachers and leaders share a state secret – that when they expect high performance of their charges they increase the likelihood of high performance.
>
> John Gardner

While it is commonly accepted that good coaches inspire athletes to produce peak performances and that parents often motivate children to excel beyond their years, the implication is that managers must do the same if they are to get their staff on board with the real challenges for the future. Some of the ways in which managers can raise individual and group expectations are by communicating an exciting vision for the future, setting clear standards and getting their staff to set challenging rather than incremental goals.

In addition, studies clearly show that successful people in all walks of life are empowered not so much through an incremental process, but by taking on demanding and sometimes risky job challenges which develop their confidence in dealing with instability and change in the future. Some of the most common experiences reported by successful middle managers include:

- being thrown in at the deep end;
- having to clear up a mess;
- being assigned a major challenge;

- taking a career risk;
- having to get results to a tight deadline;
- having to make presentations to senior managers.

PUSHING BACK THE MONKEYS

One of the major time traps for managers is being overwhelmed by the volume of problems that come from below. Contrary to the view that delegation is a top-down process, most delegation is in fact upwards: of problems, crises and interruption. Not only do managers waste a great deal of their time responding to "monkeys" from their staff, but their staff learn little from the process except that the next time they have a similar problem to refer it straight back to the manager.

> **WORD TO THE WISE**
> By solving problems for your staff you unconsciously reward them for coming with more problems.

Keeping "monkeys" with subordinates is critical to preventing the levels of reverse delegation which see managers spending much of their time on minor issues and their staff learning very little about taking extra responsibility.

A FEW SIMPLE RULES CAN HELP TO KEEP THE MONKEYS AT BAY

- Encourage your staff to come with solutions rather than problems.

- Resist giving advice – instead ask questions (e.g. "What do you suggest?" or "What are the options?").

- Have daily or weekly staff meetings at which

issues can be raised and dealt with by the group.

- Have a time in the day when you are not willing to be interrupted by staff.

- Agree procedures for dealing with recurring problems.

- Make time to train your staff and only be available for support after that.

- Reward your staff for solving their own problems.

While most managers complain about their over-work and stress, many staff complain about how little their abilities and potential are used by their managers. In a study of first-line managers 25 per cent reported using only a third of their abilities and over half said they were using between 30 and 60 per cent of their skills. If the well-worn epithet "people are our greatest asset" is to become a reality then managers have to find ways to translate the time they spend doing things themselves into "quality time", aimed at developing the confidence and abilities of their staff. Only by letting go of the urgent and routine tasks and sharing real responsibility with others can managers hope to get the time they need to address the uncertain and critical challenges in their own jobs.

REMEMBER

DO:

- Delegate real responsibility to others by making time to clarify what you want, to get ownership and to monitor and reward performance.

- Schedule time for delegation and motivation, otherwise they will not happen.

- Develop your staff by finding opportunities to stretch them, by encouraging risk taking and showing confidence in their abilities so they learn and grow in the job.

DO NOT:

- Entertain your staff with problems, get them to take ownership for their monkeys.

Chapter 7

Confront Your Indecision And Delay

This chapter will help you to:

- recognise indecision and delay as major blocks to personal effectiveness;

- see ways to challenge your delay by using six basic strategies for unblocking procrastination;

- confront the self-imposed obstacles to achievement as a manager.

Confront Your Indecision And Delay

Sometimes described as "the art of keeping up with yesterday", the habits of delay and indecision are often the result of having difficult choices to make with time. Indecision is frequently caused by having two equally good alternatives or two equally unpalatable choices to make, so we end up making no choice at all. In the story of the "Imperfect Bride", the cautious suitor makes a list of all the desirable and undesirable characteristics of his long-standing girlfriend only to find an equal number of positives and negatives. Every time he finds something that might tip things in favour of a marriage proposal, another equally convincing negative arrives to restore the balance. Eventually she makes the decision and finds someone else.

Martin is not untypical of the managers in his company. He gets in at 8.30 am and busies himself for the first half hour checking the computer, voice mail and e-mail and dealing with correspondence. Another half hour is taken up responding to messages and queries from his staff before grabbing a coffee and making his way to a meeting that takes him up to lunch time. The afternoon is similarly packed with a tight agenda – and once again he leaves the office at 6.30 pm with next year's budget in his briefcase as homework. But, instead of getting into it that evening, after a well-earned meal, he slumps into a chair in front of the television, anxious but unable to summon up the energy for a task that he's been putting off for the last two weeks. Will it get done in the same frenzy as last year?

Why do people procrastinate on some things and then end up doing them in a rush at the last minute? It is a myth that people work best under pressure, most of us work less well when we are anxious, and what excuse do you have if there was a month to get something done and at the last minute you fall sick

WORD TO THE WISE
Through indecision and delay managers often guarantee what they most fear – failure.

or find you lack a vital piece of data? In their anxiety about doing things less than perfectly, some people just do not start them at all, or start them too late to ensure that they are done any other way than badly.

Most procrastination is a response to the stress that accompanies difficult or challenging tasks and, like many reactions to stress, it can become a habit and difficult to reverse. Some of the common tasks that suffer from delay and indecision are listed below. Which do you recognise as the subject of your own procrastination?

• Writing reports or speeches.
• Carrying out performance reviews.
• Confronting difficult people.
• Starting projects.
• Getting things up to date, e.g. filing.
• Doing regular returns, e.g. budgets, forecasts, tax.
• Reading reports or journals.
• Completing paperwork.
• Filling in forms.
• Chasing people up for things.
• Actioning the outcome of meetings.
• Answering e-mail or voice mail.
• Writing up minutes.
• Asking for resources or assistance.
• Challenging those who waste your time.

Not everyone procrastinates on the same things, which suggests that the habit of delay is a response to tasks that may have been stressful in the past; and, like all bad habits, there are things you can do to start unblocking and managing them more effectively. Six useful approaches to tackling procrastination and indecision are easily remembered as the six Ds of delay.

- Do it.
- Delegate it.
- Drop it.
- Decimate it.
- Deadline it.
- Dramatise it.

DO IT

On way to tackle the habit of delay is doing something immediately to break the deadlock. Newton's law of inertia, which suggests that bodies which are at rest tend to remain at rest, equally suggests that bodies which are in motion tend to remain in motion.

Make it the big *A* for today. We often recognise our procrastination in tasks that go from one list to another list, or are relegated to the back end of the afternoon. One way to tackle your procrastination is to make them a big *A* and commit yourself to getting them off the list today. Plan to do things on which you delay early in the day and in that way they cease to be a continuing source of anxiety and act as an energiser for the rest of the day.

Use 10-minute stepping stones. As a way of reducing the anxiety that binds you to delay, commit to spending ten minutes right now to doing something on a difficult task. Take ten minutes to draw up a plan of action for the task, or break the task into bits and schedule time for each piece in your diary, or put deadlines on each of the chunks. Doing ten minutes on something you have been putting off for a few days is often enough to see the wood for the trees.

Get some data. One major obstacle to getting started on some things is the lack of information to write that report, answer a letter or schedule a job review. Break the back of procrastination today by getting some data on the task, spending half an hour reading a report, getting out the relevant documents, ringing up a few people for information, printing out some computer files or simply doing up a list of the information you need to start the project. Making time to get information is often enough to feel energised about a task where you feel uncertain or anxious.

DELEGATE IT

One way to rid yourself of things that cause anxiety in your day is to give them to some one else who may find them less stressful and more challenging.

Share your anxiety. If there are things on which you are delaying because you do not like doing them, share the concern with others as a way of getting in touch with your own anxiety: "I hate doing these returns", "I'm really uncomfortable about presenting at that meeting". Not only does sharing a concern help to reduce the anxiety, but someone, who finds the task less onerous or actually enjoys doing it, may volunteer to help you with it.

Have faith in others. We are sometimes reluctant to give things to our staff because we do not trust their willingness or feel they lack the skills. Yet ask any person about their peak career experiences and for most it was being given something that really stretched them. Most people, when trusted to do something by their boss, will go to great lengths to do it well. As General Patton once said: "Don't tell people how to do things, just tell them what to do and you will be surprised with the results."

Get others to nag. Rather than delegating a difficult task you could delegate the monitoring process. One of the best ways to get progress on some things is to let others know that you are trying to finish a report, complete a project, give up smoking or lose weight and get them to remind you about your commitment. In getting this book finished, I have been helped by a couple of friends who regularly asked me: "How is the book going?", "How many chapters have you done?", "When will it be finished?"

> **WORD TO THE WISE**
> Not everything is worth doing now; some things are better left for the future or not done at all.

DROP IT

Rather than force of habit blocking progress on difficult tasks, it is often lack of energy that prevents us from getting into the big things. Some things are hard to start because there isn't a deadline or a crisis to drive us into action and so it goes from one list to another in the hope that in time we will find the energy to begin.

De-list it. We put some tasks onto lists even though we have no real energy to do them. If a task has appeared on a number of your 'to do' lists, then one option is to simply cross it off; if it is important it will find a way to get back onto the list in the future when you may have more energy to deal with it. Remember that some things are not worth doing at all and some things are not worth doing right now.

Schedule it for the future. If a particular task is something you want to do but do not have the time or the energy right now, one option is to schedule it for the future. If you are under pressure for the next couple of weeks, put a note in your diary to trigger that task at a future date when you are likely to be less hassled or to see it as another source of anxiety.

Do up a worry list. Sometimes putting your concerns on paper is enough to see them differently. After you have drawn up a list of the things on which you have been delaying, consign it to a desk drawer or, better still, put it up on the wall so you can occasionally re-check your concerns. Do a periodic worry list to see that the things you worried about last month were actioned or done in some other way. Also, console yourself with the thought that if you weren't worried about these things you would probably be worried about something else.

DECIMATE IT

Some things in life we keep putting off because they are big and long-term, hard to start and difficult to finish. Most projects have an uncertain beginning because they are unclear and ambiguous and a great deal of energy can be lost during a project if the progress is slow or there is no end in sight.

Chunk the elephants. Sometimes big tasks are hard to manage because they demand a time commitment that isn't readily available. One way of dealing with those things is to break them into smaller chunks. Even if you have already broken a project into chunks, break them into even smaller bits as a way of getting started.

As part of the management team, John had part of the strategic plan to complete for the next management meeting. He knew it would take a couple of days and, although there was ten days to go, he had been putting it off for the past few weeks. He finally got some momentum into the job by breaking it into bits and picking three small tasks to do tomorrow. He also scheduled four separate hours into his diary for getting the bigger chunks completed. Two days later he felt a sense of relief at his progress and much more energy for the challenge.

Breaking things into small chunks often makes them easier to action, it also allows you to get a number of small successes rather than one big success; and it is short-term successes that create and sustain energy to go on to the more difficult chunks of larger projects.

Clock the hours. One way to break the inertia on bigger tasks is to chunk them into hours and work to the clock.   When the author James Thurber was finding it difficult to put pen to paper, his long-suffering wife Althea encouraged him to set an alarm clock to ring in 45 minutes and to force himself to have something written by the time it went off – he did and it cured his writers' block. Many things get done if you treat them as a series of time commitments and plan to get something done in each hour.

Figure 7.1: Time Planner

If there is a major task you have been avoiding for a while get into it by identifying the amount of time you need to give each week to ensure its completion by the deadline. Set a specific goal, and as you complete an hour or half an hour, record it against the goal.

Goals - 6 hours a week for next 6 weeks or XYZ project					
Weeks 1	2	3	4	5	6
Hours ✓	✓	✓	✓	✓	✓
✓	✓	✓	✓	✓	✓
✓	✓	✓	✓	✓	✓
✓	✓	✓	✓	✓	✓
	✓	✓	✓	✓	✓
		✓	✓	✓	
		✓		✓	
		✓		✓	
4	5	8	6	8	5

Schedule procrastination for peak hours. Do things on which you delay at times of the day when you have your best energy. For the average person that is early on in the day – between 8.00 am and 11.00 am for over 85 per cent of managers. Apart from getting an early success, you will also be working on the difficult things at times of the day when you have most energy. Leaving difficult things until the back end of the day or taking them home in a briefcase, simply adds to the problem by trying to get energy for them at times of the day you are most likely to see them as onerous jobs.

Identify a couple of tasks you have been postponing for the past few weeks; it could be a budget, writing a report or dealing with a difficult issue. Use your diary to schedule an hour or two for them this week in your peak time. While working on them in your peak energy hour is no guarantee of success, at least you will be giving them your best shot by attacking them when you have your best mental energy. And a couple of concentrated hours on most major tasks is usually enough to see them as manageable.

DEADLINE IT

Most projects become troublesome because your energy starts to wane half way through the process – many people who succeed in life, whether athletes, writers or entrepreneurs, simply persist a little longer.

Use mini-deadlines. While putting a completion date on a project gives you a target to aim for, it is usually too far in the future to provide any immediate energy, the reason that many people wait for an impending deadline to spur them into action. It helps to make energy for deadlines if you break them into bits and put a mini-deadline on each part of the project.

How do major projects get to be late – One day at a time.

Tom Peters

Make deadlines visible by putting them in your diary, or on the wall as a reminder of your commitment, and use mini-deadlines to move you on to the next stage – even if you haven't completed this stage to your satisfaction. Aiming for perfection usually means that projects drift over time, whereas meeting the deadline, even if not to your complete satisfaction, gives you a sense of success and usually there is time to go back on the bits you need to tidy up.

When I was doing a research degree some years ago, my supervisor was at a university 400 miles away. It took a plane, two train journeys and a taxi to get from where I lived to our six weekly meetings. Between each visit I worked long and hard to justify the expense and time involved in each trip so that it would not be a wasted journey. If we had lived a couple of miles apart we would probably have met more frequently, but there would also have been far less need to achieve the kind of progress that was generated by those six weekly deadlines.

Monitor tasks with mini-events. It often helps to break the cycle of under-achievement and loss of energy on projects if you break them into chunks and recognise your progress at the end of each chunk. Mini-events might include making a short progress presentation to your peers, rewarding yourself with a break or, better still, rewarding someone like your spouse or staff if you come in on time with a stage of the project.

DRAMATISE IT

Some tasks are put on the long finger because they are boring, routine or seemingly endless. One way to generate some energy for those kind of jobs is to make them more challenging and fun.

Chunk the boredom. While some jobs are neither urgent or important, they still have to get done. But because they are boring, we often let the paperwork or filing pile up on the desk until it becomes a time consuming and frustrating task.

One way of dealing with routine or boring jobs is to chunk the boredom into half hour segments. Schedule two half hour slots this week in your diary for paperwork, preferably in the afternoons since it requires less mental energy. Do an occasional blitz on your filing by letting it pile up for a couple of weeks and scheduling two hours each month to get it up to date. Try sorting your paperwork into three files, urgent, important and routine. Read the routine pile once and do something with it – preferably file it in the bin. Schedule some time in the future to deal with the important paperwork and put the urgent stuff on your 'to do' list for today.

Make boring tasks into games. Most games are attractive because they contain an element of challenge. One woman who hates doing housework starts her day by inspecting the house and putting post-it notes in areas that require her attention. As she completes each task she removes the note and puts it on her kitchen notice board – the challenge is to see how many notes she can collect before the deadline of 11.00 am. A successful female executive has a flip chart in her office and a series of post-it notes on the left-hand side with the jobs she has to complete that day. As she completes each task she moves the note to the right side of the board, letting herself and others see the progress she is making.

I once saw a couple of labourers fixing parking buffers in a car park. The buffers were short slabs of concrete fixed to the tarmac surface with two metal spikes. The two labourers had made a boring job into a game by timing each other hammering the spikes into the ground: and I am sure they had more than a gentleman's wager on the result.

Promise yourself a reward. Start your day by identifying the three most important tasks for today, and promise yourself a reward for each task completed, such as a break, a wander around or an early lunch. On longer term tasks, promise yourself something a bit more interesting like a trip to the theatre or a weekend away and be a ruthless judge of your own efforts.

Make your procrastination into fun. Some things are easier to handle if the heat is taken out of them. Many organisations recognise the benefits of having dress down days once a week or month when staff come to work in casual clothes for a concentrated day of office work or internal meetings. Vary the locations of your routine meetings as a way of making them more fun – have some standing up, in the canteen or outdoors. Consider having the occasional off-site meeting at a hotel to look at the big picture or to encourage creativity, and include a break for physical activity or a team challenge.

The management activity most subject to procrastination is planning – it goes by the board if there is a crisis and much of it gets done outside working hours. One way to get more time for planning is to make it fun; try staying at home one morning a month to review your results and plan for the next period; try more creative approaches to planning, such as doing drawings of the future, having a half hour brainstorm with a couple of colleagues or taking a thoughtful walk. If you need time to read reports or journals, do it in the park or the lobby of a hotel. Plan things, such as job reviews on train journeys, have planning meetings in a local cafe and hold competitions to get creative suggestions for improving service or delivery.

Many things conspire to get in the way of what we are trying to achieve as managers, and chief among them is ourselves. Although some of the habits we develop for coping with work overload or anxiety are useful, others only add to the feelings of pressure and under achievement. While it is sometimes good to delay things or let your subconscious work on decisions overnight, if it is getting in the way of what you want to achieve in your job, then do something to break the habits that may be feeding your procrastination or replace your bad habits with better and more productive routines. Procrastination really is the thief of time.

REMEMBER

DO:

- Start taking more ownership for your procrastination.

- Something now to break the inertia of indecision and delay.

- Use one of the six strategies for breaking the stranglehold of delay – do it, delegate it, drop it, decimate it, deadline it or dramatise it.

- Make daily procrastination into a big *A* and break the baby elephants into smaller and more manageable pieces.

DO NOT:

- Let fear of failure get in the way of your effectiveness.

Chapter 8

Minimise The Daily Distractions

This chapter will help you to:

- see that managers collude and encourage many of the time wasters about which they complain;
- identify creative solutions to your chronic time wasters;
- develop a stategy for dealing with the time robbers at work.

Minimise The Daily Distractions

Although managing time means making better choices and finding ways to focus on the real challenges in the job, a lot of things get in the way of what managers want to get done with their day. Apart from the routine work they should be giving to others and the tasks that are subject to personal delay, managers have to deal with a volume of time wasters that come at the rate of one every six minutes and account for upwards of 20-30 per cent of their time – one day every week.

**Figure 8.1: Top Ten Time Wasters:
Rank Order (220 managers)**

- Telephone.
- Saying "no".
- Day to day crises.
- Having to chase others up.
- Drop-in visitors.
- Personal disorganisation.
- Being too available.
- Procrastination.
- Correspondence and paperwork.
- Ad hoc and regular meetings.

Not only do managers spend a substantial amount of their time dealing with daily distractions but the cumulative effect of those minor derailments, which may only take a few minutes here or there, can add up to a major block to getting the important tasks done.

COLLUSION AND CURE

A few illuminating comments on the nature of time wasters helps to see them for what they are.

1. You cannot eliminate time wasters altogether because many of them go with the job – but to manage effectively you do need to minimise the effect of constant distractions, such as the telephone or drop-ins.

2. At best managers collude in their time wasters. They learn to live in an atmosphere that is characterised by telephone interruptions and minor crises and would miss many of them if they were absent – wouldn't it be a dull old day if the telephone never rang or there was no correspondence or drop in visitors? Be honest.

3. Not only do managers collude in their time wasters, they actually encourage some of them as a way of avoiding the more important tasks. How often have you dropped in to someone else's office or made a few telephone calls as a way of avoiding a job that is sitting on your desk that you don't want to start? How often have you allowed yourself to be sidetracked by the easy things on your 'to do' list as a way of avoiding the ones you know are the most difficult?

4. Managers blame many of their time wasters on other people. "Attribution theory" suggests that it is part of the human condition to blame our failures on others and to claim successes for ourselves. Many managers, who complain about the volume of telephone interruptions in their day, also carry a mobile phone everywhere they go, respond immediately to the telephone and encourage others to call them on the slightest of pretexts. Managers who complain about the number of drop-ins frequently have an open-door policy, comfortable chairs to encourage the sitters and body language which suggests that casual visitors are more then welcome to interrupt.

Of course some time wasters are in the nature of the business – or are they? If, as a manager, you are spending an inordinate amount of time dealing with distractions and minor issues in the day then you are probably not achieving what you are there to achieve. While you may be inclined to blame others for wasting your time you also have to take responsibility for colluding in them and start to take ownership for minimising their effects.

CHRONIC TIME WASTERS

Breaking time wasting habits is difficult because, like long hours or taking work home many of them are chronic, and chronic habits are hard to break. Most managers have already tried the usual prescriptions for dealing with time wasters and found they haven't worked. Rather than steeling yourself to remedies that have failed in the past, you have to start looking for creative ways to break the habits that waste your time.

One simple process for identifying creative solutions is brainstorming, which has three simple rules.

1. Take five minutes to list all the creative solutions you can think of to one of your major time wasters. As well as the practical solutions, also look for the wild or extreme possibilities. (Try it as a group exercise on a shared time waster, such as meetings or paperwork – two or three heads are more creative than one.)

2. Do not edit what you write down. Put everything on the list no matter how ridiculous it may seem.

3. Now pick the most 'practical idea' from the list and the 'wildest idea'. Although the practical idea may seem more likely to succeed, often the

wildest idea presents the seed of a better solution. At a recent brainstorming session, one of the suggestions for dealing with telephone interruptions was to put the phone in a bucket of water. The idea of cooling down the phone suggested taking it off the hook for an hour each day, getting away from it if there is something you want to finish or rotating the handling of telephone queries so that everyone takes a turn.

At all levels, there are creative ideas that suggest solutions to chronic time wasters. As CEO of IBM, Frank Carey cut down the amount of time taken up at meetings with ill-conceived proposals by insisting that all ideas be expressed on a single sheet of paper. A senior manager in a small company, who spends two days a week away from the office, found that his staff had developed the convenient habit of leaving their problems on his desk on pieces of paper. He often came back to the office to find a minor mound of paper that contributed little to his effectiveness. His solution was to remove his desk from the office so that people had no place to leave the paper. It worked so well that he introduced a paperless office – the rule was that no piece of paper came into his office without going out again.

Faced with the problem of winter icing on cables, which was costing a fortune in repairs and seriously affecting customer service, a North American electricity supplier used brainstorming to come up with ideas for resolving the issue. One of the wild ideas was to string pots of honey along the cables to encourage hungry bears to climb the pylons and in so doing to dislodge the ice. Further visions of "a bear in the air" lead to the possibility of using the down draft of a helicopter to dislodge ice from the cabling. That relatively simple solution ended up saving thousands of dollars a year for the company in reduced repairs and unbroken service.

As you examine the solutions to your major time wasters be aware of your own tendency to dismiss the more creative and imaginative ideas with phrases such as "that wouldn't work" or "I couldn't get away with it". Killing off creative ideas (ideacide) is the way in which we deny possibilities for improving things – in the same way that insurance companies condemned customers to lengthy applications until someone came up with the idea of direct telephone sales, or that caused mainframe computer companies to dismiss the PC as a crazy idea until someone saw otherwise.

CREATIVE SOLUTIONS

At the risk of adding to the list of handy hints for resolving time wasters, here are some creative solutions for minimising the more common distractions in your day.

Detach yourself from the Phone

Without doubt, the biggest disrupter in the day is the telephone. With its insistent ring and potential for surprise, most people cannot resist answering it even if they are in the middle of something much more important. No matter how long the line in a bank or airline office the telephone gets precedence – at meetings serious issues are set aside while someone rushes from the room to take the most trivial of calls on their mobile. On a recent television chat show one of the guests even interrupted the interviewer to take a call from her mother.

One way to start reducing the invasiveness of the telephone is by logging the content and duration of

your calls over two to three days –
you may find that many of them
could have been redirected or handled in a shorter time. Have a
"quiet time" in the day when you
are not willing to be interrupted. In
the same way that some companies
have introduced dress down days,
why not have a telephone free

morning, a few hours in the week when all internal
calls are banned and voice-mail messages are taken
for external calls.

Start to reply to calls at times of the day when
you expect to get the other person's voicemail; it
ensures they got the message and the call is brief.
Use the 20/80 principle on calls – decide who you
want to receive calls from and get a message on the
others. Finally, if you cannot hide the interruptions,
then hide yourself. Work in someone else's office for
those couple of hours you need for thinking or planning or start working from home one day a month
to write reports or do a blitz on your reading.

Say "No" and Mean It

Why do people frequently say "yes" to things and
then later regret it? We partly say "yes" to avoid the
guilt that goes with saying "no", even if it is at great
expense to our own work. Also, most people have
difficulty saying "no" to things that are in the future
– if someone wants to meet or visit you next month
you are more likely to say "yes" than if the same
person wanted to meet with you right now.

At a practical level, it is usually much easier to
say "no" if you are certain about what you want to
get done with your time. Having the clear focus of
long-term priorities, a 'to do' list and scheduled
diary commitments on major tasks makes it much
easier to fend off the time stealers. It is also easier

to say "no" if you practice being assertive, using "I" statements (such as "I'm sorry but I have to finish this by 4.00 pm") while at the same time making eye contact and using body language that is forceful.

Draw up a list of the things on which you want to start saying "no" and record the times you are successful. Before making commitments to others, give yourself the breathing space of getting back to the office or sleep on it overnight –

> **WORD TO THE WISE**
> Stress is often the result of your brain saying "no" and your mouth saying "I'll see what I can do".

a good night's rest is often enough to convince you to say "no" to something that could so easily have wasted your time. Pick a role model who is assertive with their time and adopt a couple of their habits. Punish people who want to dump their problems on you by sending them away with one of yours and hounding them for a response. Reward yourself for saying "no" and make the reward unusual, such as a trip to an art gallery or buying a new pair of shoes, or, alternatively, just stop responding to some people so quickly or at all – get a reputation for not being a soft touch.

Reduce the Daily Crises

Day to day crises usually take the form of minor problems from a variety of sources including your boss, staff, colleagues or customers. Most of them aren't novel, they have happened before and as such lend themselves to being made into procedures or delegated. As minor crises on aeroplanes or at theme parks are handled by the most junior of staff, get some pleasure from watching your staff taking responsibility for the crises and reward them as an encouragement to continue their efforts. Also, reward others, such as your boss, for going to your staff in the first instance: "You will find Jim is a real expert in this area." When a problem comes onto your desk the first question you should always ask is: "Why me?" Before responding to any issue consider whether it is urgent or whether someone else could do it – most crises aren't that critical and could probably be handled by a number of people. If it has to be handled by you, then see it as an opportunity to deal with things differently in the future – set aside time to train others in crisis handling or monitor issues that have a potential for becoming problems in the future.

Control your Chasing Up

One of the consequences of relying on others for results is the amount of chasing up you may have to do to get them to meet the deadline. Managers often compound the problem by doing it themselves or establishing a norm that things aren't urgent until they have reminded people at least a couple of times.

One of the best ways to get others to deliver on their promises is to nag them, either by confronting the individual each time you see them, grabbing them first thing in the morning, sitting in their office until you get an answer or delegating the "nagging" to someone else who may get a better response.

When Alan Ladd Jnr was at United Artists he wanted to re-employ a technician on a consultancy arrangement. Ladd was being put through the usual difficulties by personnel and wanted his boss to put pressure on them to make a decision, but with little success. Before he left on a two week business commitment he dictated fourteen memos to his secretary with the instruction that she should send one of them to his boss each day with the same request: "Have you go the decision yet?"

At the end of his trip he came back to a positive response.

Use reverse psychology, praising those who deliver on time, or alternatively stop nagging the worst offenders and let a crisis occur so they can see that you are not going to chase them up every time.

Discourage the Drop Ins

People who waste your time with casual or frequent interruption aren't too much of a problem unless there is something more important on your desk. But instead of telling them to go away, managers often collude in the interruption with an open door and an absence of feedback that might indicate they are less than welcome. As a result they end up working late to get something done that they could have got done in the day.

Try using discussion enders to bring casual conversations to a close: "Is that it?" or "Was there something else?" If that doesn't work be more assertive: "I have to get this in the post by lunch time" or just walk out of the room and leave them sitting. If it is your boss who keeps interrupting, think of regularising a weekly meeting or touching base at a time in the day that suits you. Also, let them know how the important things are going – they are entitled to know if something they delegated is being done or has run into trouble. If you are undertaking a project for your boss give them regular progress reports so they know you are on schedule and won't be embarrassed if someone asks how the project is going.

If your staff are the main interrupters, adopt the policy of not accepting their "monkeys" – send them away to do some thinking rather than giving them solutions which may encourage them to keep coming back. Get them to put the problem in writing or assure them of your support in whatever they decide and keep letting them know the problem is theirs, not yours. Also, regularise daily or weekly meetings so that issues can be left until the meeting rather than encouraging them to drop in at inconvenient times of the day.

Have a closed-door policy for part of your day – hide where people are less likely to get you, or put a notice on your door for an hour saying: "Do Not Disturb" and do not add "please", which makes it conditional on the person deciding whether the interruption is important enough.

Getting to Grips with the Time Robbers

Time wasters are hard to tackle because many of them go with the job. They are also part of the buzz of working in organisations and, as such, create variety for managers who like them all the more for that. In certain cases, time wasters can also be used as work avoidance techniques (WATS) providing managers with a convenient cover for things they are reluctant to start.

Managing time wasters isn't so much a question of eliminating all the distractions in your day, but minimising them – at times you may have little alternative but to answer the phone or to drop everything and handle a crisis. However, if they continue to prevent you from achieving what you want to get done in the day then you do have to find ways to control them.

As a strategy for breaking the habits that feed your time wasters the following approaches can help.

1. **Make sure you keep focused on the important things**. If you have daily and weekly priorities for which you are making time it is much easier to let go of the habits that sustain your time wasting.

2. **Identify the main time leaks in the job**. Get in

touch with the things that frustrate your efforts, the interruptions that fragment your day or the tasks that take up your time and contribute little to your effectiveness. If a particular time waster accounts for a chunk of the problem, then get some data on the number of interruptions, their duration and impact. Set a goal to reduce the time you spend on specific time wasters and have an action plan for implementing it.

3. **Replace some of your bad habits with good habits**. Reduce the number of minor crises or interruptions from your staff by having regular meetings or monthly one on ones. Replace the habit of allowing the telephone to interrupt you on important tasks by completing those tasks away from the phone or at lunch time. Have a quiet time in the day when you let the answer machine take messages – even leave a recorded message so people will know when you will be available.

4. **Look for more creative ways to reduce the time wasters**. Recognise that the remedies you have already tried aren't working and you need to do something different, preferably more creative on the basis that most habits are chronic. Many companies have adopted creative approaches to some of the more common time wasters by having stand up meetings, insisting on one page memos, having an hour of quiet time in the day and establishing dress down days. The unusual is now becoming a more acceptable way for managers to work.

Managing the time leaks doesn't mean eliminating everything that gets in the way of your effectiveness – some time wasters should be enjoyed for what they are – opportunities to reflect, a break from the stress or a chance to network with colleagues.

However getting to grips with the time robbers does mean changing your locus of control away from believing there is nothing you can do to influence them, to recognising that you can minimise their effect. Some things in the day have to be done but not to the extent that we end up doing them, and some time wasters are a choice, to be available, to procrastinate, to set unrealistic estimates and to entertain drop-ins. Managing the time wasters in your day also means learning to be more ruthless with your time if you really want to get progress on the important things – start to take a bit more responsibility for controlling the things that can so easily end up controlling you.

REMEMBER

DO:

- Acknowledge the fact that you cannot eliminate time wasters altogether but you can minimise them.

- Do something creative to start managing the major time wasters.

- Look for the practical solutions that are often contained in the wildest idea.

DO NOT:

- Collude with your time wasters by accepting or encouraging them.

Chapter 9

De-stress The Work Pressure

This chapter will help you to:

- recognise the job and personality stressors at work;
- identify the main symptoms of job-related stress;
- develop practical ways of relieving daily stressors in the job;
- plan to control the longer term causes of stress.

De-stress The Work Pressure

Managing time is about making choices, to focus on the important things and finding ways to manage the others. But making difficult choices isn't easy or relaxing – give a child a bar of chocolate and they will eat it, give them the choice of one thing in the sweet shop and they are immediately showing symptoms of stress. Much of the stress at work comes from the way managers react to the many difficult and often confusing choices in the job – while some respond to the daily pressures by making better choices with their time others try to beat their way out of over commitment by working even longer hours to catch up with the increasing backlog.

EU-STRESS AND DISTRESS

Not all stress is bad stress. Eu-stress ('eu' stands for euphoria) is the kind of stress that leads people to peak performance, helps them respond to crises and adapt to change, and some managers need more of it in the job. But the negative side of stress, which we often recognise in ourselves, is the result of a continuous and unrelenting pressure that pushes us beyond our ability to adapt and leads to anxiety, exhaustion and sometimes burnout.

The Job Stressors

Some stress comes from the type of jobs we are in and some from the kind of people we are. The most common job stressors include:

- continuous and tight deadlines;
- job overload;
- long hours;
- fire fighting rather than working to a plan;

- role ambiguity and conflict;
- inadequately trained staff;
- constant, negative feedback.

A great deal of the job stress that managers experience can be summed up in one word 'overwork'. Under constant pressure to improve results against increasing competition and with limited resources, the 2-3-2 formula suggests that in today's environment half the people are doing three times the work for twice the pay. One recent survey shows that two out of every five managers are working more than 50 hours a week and one in eight managers are doing more than 60 hours, not including travel or taking work home. The pressure on people to work longer and harder is further reflected in a recent survey of UK office workers which found that 25 per cent take a lunch break of less than 30 minutes, 20 per cent regularly skip their lunch and 2 per cent go without lunch altogether.

The Personality Stressors

While stress comes from the types of job we do, it also comes from the kind of people we are and the way we respond to pressure in the job. In a classic study on stress and personality, Drs Roseman and Friedman looked at 3,500 healthy men and their response to stress conditions. On the basis of their lifestyle and ways of coping with pressure the researchers classified them as *Type A* and *Type B* personalities, and predicted that the *Type A*s would suffer more heart attacks than *Type B*s. Over the ten year period of the study 250 of the group suffered coronaries of whom 85 per cent were *Type A* personalities.

Type A	Type B
Very competitive	Not competitive
Strong, forceful	Easy-going manner
Does everything quickly	Methodical

Ambitious	Moderately ambitious
Impatient	Not upset by delays
Very conscious of time	Not conscious of time
Restless when inactive	Enjoys periods of inactivity

While *Type A* managers are go-getters, intolerant of delay and incompetence, are always ready to assume responsibility and tend to work better when they are up against tight deadlines, the *Type Bs* tend to be more placid, task-oriented and slower to anger. Although most people are a mixture of both types, many successful managers would tend towards a *Type A* personality.

SYMPTOMS AND CAUSES

However, whether you are working in a stressful environment or have to live with a stressful personality, it isn't so much the pressure that causes the problems but the way you respond to the stress. Some useful habits for coping with pressure at work are suggested by examining three broad strategies for dealing with stress: responding to the symptoms, reducing the daily effects of time pressure and removing the root causes.

Recognise the Symptoms

Organisational life doesn't cause stress, just stress conditions. When people first experience the effects of continuous work pressure, they often dismiss the symptoms as temporary, expecting them to disappear, when the pressure is relieved or disguised with self-medication. When the symptoms re-appear, the tendency is to rationalise them as part of the job or see them as personal weaknesses rather than as warning signals of a longer term condition. Left unchecked, the initial signals of stress can lead to more persistent and pernicious conditions, such as hypertension and arthritis, and other serious diseases which research is only beginning to link with stress, such as asthma, diabetes and cancer.

Initial Stress Signals

Physical	Emotional
Fatigue	Anxiety
Sleep problems	Feeling of being out of control
Muscle aches	Withdrawal from others
Indigestion	Loss of concentration
Headaches	Inability to relax
Palpitations	Loss of self-worth
Skin rashes	Concern about health

Figure 9.1: Stress Facts

- A CBI Survey shows 30-40 per cent of absences from work are due to stress.

- 90 million days are lost each year in the UK through stress.

- In Sweden, the cost of heart disease due to stress is 3,190 million ECU.

- 1 in 20 workers suffer from depressive illnesses in Ireland.

- In the US over $295 million worth of tranquillisers are consumed each year and $195 million is spent on sleeping pills.

While stress is mainly associated with the negative side of work pressure, it is also associated with success. Executive "burnout", which is defined as the accumulation of stress over time shows no obvious symptoms in the short-term, but in the long-term can leave its victims psychologically disabled with feelings of anger, helplessness, of being trapped in the job, disillusioned with their careers and putting increasing effort into maintaining the hectic pace they have set for themselves. According to Dr Freudenberger who popularised the concept of "burnout", the typical candidate is "dynamic, charismatic and goal-oriented", a pretty accurate description of many successful managers.

Figure 9.2: How Burned Out Are You?

How often do these things apply to you?
seldom=1, sometimes=2, often=3, very often=4

1. I do not feel rested or relaxed.
2. I feel no sense of accomplishment.
3. I worry about the future.
4. I feel trapped.
5. My work isn't interesting.
6. I have poor communication with others.
7. There is never enough time to do things correctly.
8. The work is just too hard.
9. I get no support from others.
10. My co-workers are always complaining.
11. I ache and feel less than well.
12. I regret lost opportunities.
13. I have no sense of direction.
14. I have low self-esteem.
15. My co-workers are unco-operative.

Total Score:

Interpretation of the Scores:
39-60:   burned out
34-38:   likely to burn out
29-33:   initial symptoms of burn out
24-28:   OK
15-23:   doing fine

REDUCE THE DAILY STRESSORS

While the more traditional approaches to stress management emphasise removing the causes of work pressure or changing the job conditions, others focus on reducing the daily effects of working in a stressful environment. When you feel harassed, under pressure or out of control in the day, rather than trying to beat your way out of it, do something to relieve the effects.

WORD TO THE WISE
Organisations do not cause stress, just stress conditions; it is the way you respond that causes the stress.

Take a breather. When people are anxious they often take short and shallow breaths. Not only does this restrict their oxygen supply, but it also results in an increase of carbon dioxide to the bloodstream, constricts the blood vessels, reduces oxygen supply, to the brain and adds to the feelings of tension and panic. One simple way to relieve anxiety during the day is to take three or four deep breaths whenever you feel anxious, drawing in as much air as you can, and as you exhale say the word "relax", silently. By focusing on your body you take the tension off your mind.

Have frequent stretch breaks. When they are under pressure, many people experience tightening of the muscle endings which results in unspecific aches and overall body stiffness. Taking a stretch break every hour, by tightening up and loosening each muscle in turn, can help relieve those symptoms. Start by pulling your toes towards your knees and holding it for the count of ten. Feel the tension in the backs of your legs. Now, relax and feel the tension go. Do the same with your thighs and so on up to your face opening your mouth wide and stretching your chin as far as it will go to the count of ten. Feel the tension disappear and then relax for a few minutes.

Take a nap. Many well-known figures have found that taking a short nap is a convenient antidote to daily fatigue. Celebrity nappers have included Albert Einstein, John Kennedy and Winston

Churchill, while Billy Graham still takes a nap before an important speech and Mark McCormack, business adviser to many famous sportsmen, schedules a lunch time rest as a daily commitment. In support of the afternoon nap, physiologists have recently discovered that the body's natural energy goes through a marked dip in the middle of the day, suggesting that the siesta cultures, such as Greece and Mexico, have probably got things right.

According to legend, the painter Salvador Dali took frequent naps during the day. To make sure that he didn't fall into a deeper sleep he sat in a chair, his arm hanging down with a spoon cupped loosely between his fingers. Underneath the spoon, on the floor, was a tin plate. By the time the spoon hit the floor he had dozed just enough to be refreshed by the rest.

Try a power walk. If you are tired after lunch or are in the habit of sinking into a chair after a heavy meal get into the routine of going for a brisk twenty minute walk instead. Apart from aiding digestion, a brisk walk can help to normalise blood pressure and reduce cholesterol. Power walking simply means walking at a pace that increases the metabolic rate (consumption of calories) and the heart rate, about two steps every second, the pace of a moderate hand clap.

REMOVE THE ROOT CAUSES

Most persistent stress conditions are the result of a steady build up of fatigue over time. On the basis that managing is a hazardous profession, it is sound advice for any manager to keep in good physical shape, and one of the most effective ways is regular exercise.

Practice aerobic fitness. Meaning "in the presence of oxygen", aerobic fitness requires regular exercise, at least twice a week, sufficient to increase the intake of oxygen for at least twenty minutes. The effects of aerobic exercise can be achieved through a standard workout programme or any aerobic sport (e.g. cycling, tennis, jogging, swimming or brisk walking). More important is that you exercise in a way that you enjoy rather than making it another task to be squeezed into your busy day.

> **WORD TO THE WISE**
> Only those who can pass the most rigorous physical examination can safely follow the sedentary life.
> TK Whyte

It will also help if you make a regular commitment to exercise by joining a class, blocking out specific times in your diary for exercise, involving others in the activity or keeping a chart of your progress. You can add direction to any exercise programme by making it into a challenge, such as planning to run a mini-marathon, doing a sponsored walk or placing a bet on reducing your weight. Another way of committing to healthy exercise is to replace some of your bad habits with good ones, such as scheduling a weekly tennis game, going for a swim or having a gym session straight after work as a way of encouraging you to leave the office on time.

Keep in good mental shape. Originally developed by the Maharishi Yoga as transcendental meditation (TM) the "relaxation response" was popularised among the business community by a Dr Herbert Benson. It involves two twenty minute sessions a day in which a mantra (silent sound) is repeated as a way of calming the racing thoughts that accompany anxiety and fatigue. The five steps in the relaxation response are simple and unmystical.

1. Sit in a comfortable position.

2. Close your eyes.
3 Relax your muscles one by one starting at your feet and progressing to your face. Allow them to remain relaxed.
4. Breathe through your nose and become aware of your breathing. As you breathe out say the word "one", silently to yourself and continue saying "one", at each outward breath.
5. Continue to relax for twenty minutes and when you have finished, sit quietly for a couple of minutes.

In an experiment on the benefits of the relaxation response, 80 subjects with high blood pressure were asked to meditate for twenty minutes twice a day over a 9-week period. During the experiment, their systolic and diastolic pressures fell by an average of ten millimetres, bringing them down to normal levels. Equally interesting was that those who stopped meditating after the experiment found their blood pressure soon returned to its original level.

Eat early and snack often. Many of the problems associated with fatigue and anxiety relate to poor diet. We are all familiar with the harassed manager who is on the go from early morning until late evening, consuming numerous cups of coffee, snacking on biscuits and lunching on the run. According to Dr Michael McGannon, Medical Director at INSEAD and author of *The Urban Warrior*, battling the effects of dietary fatigue should includes elements of the following action plan.

1. Go for a brisk 15-minute walk after lunch.
2. Do not mix proteins and starches, which are incompatible foods.

3. Avoid alcohol at lunch time.
4. Snack sensibly between meals, e.g. nuts, cheese, and fruit, to avoid low sugar levels.
5. Limit your coffee intake.
6. Drink two to three litres of fresh water daily – between meals.

Contrary to the myth that coffee and sugar increase your energy during the day, they can actually add to fatigue by over stimulating the adrenal glands which in turn leads to a rush of insulin and premature fatigue. The same applies to sweets or biscuits which may give you a temporary lift for about an hour but will leave you with less energy in the longer term. Also important for avoiding fatigue is that you consume most of your high energy food in the first half of the day – instead of a light breakfast of toast, cereal and coffee, the traditional breakfast that includes sugar and fat to slow down digestion is still the best. Try to avoid eating late in the evening, which is likely to reduce your ability to get a good night's sleep. The old adage "breakfast like a king, lunch like a prince and dine like a pauper" still remains pretty sound advice.

Let go of perfection. The people most susceptible to stress in the workplace are the perfectionists who want to get everything done, do not trust others and treat everything as if it were urgent and important. Perfectionists are hard on themselves, punishing their own imperfections by working harder to get everything right and denying others opportunities to relax and enjoy their work. If your perfectionism is denying you time for relaxation or enjoyment, then try to build in a few good habits to replace those which are adding to your stress.

1. Start walking to work, or part of the way, or go walking at lunch time.

2. Plan two weekend breaks with your family.
3. Delegate one job or family responsibility to someone else.
4. Track the hours you put into the job and plan to reduce them.
5. Learn to trust others by scheduling more time with your key staff.
6. Set a deadline on starting and finishing meetings – set a time limit on tasks (not everything is worth doing well).
7. Have a quiet time or relaxing twenty minute nap in the day.
8. Set aside half an hour once or twice a week to read – do it in a relaxing place like a coffee shop or a park bench.
9. Have lunch with a colleague or friend at least once a week.
10. Keep a diary to reflect and plan to do things differently.

Managing is a hazardous profession. Unlike the doctor, lawyer or teacher, a manager's success cannot be measured in the number of clients they see or the hours they spend in the classroom. They are evaluated against the results they achieve, which are often ambiguous, long-term and considerably outside their control. The danger for managers is believing that, if you work harder and longer, there is more chance of being effective or successful in the job. Working hard is no guarantee of success in managing – much more critical is identifying where you want to go for the future and focusing on the main priorities while at the same time recognising 'busyness' as one of the major blocks to effectiveness.

Managing effectively means making better choices with your time, not trying to do everything right but doing the right things right. Not only does focusing on everything mean that you are focusing on nothing it is also a recipe for long hours, frustration and stress. While managers do need occasional bouts of pressure to experience the euphoria of beating deadlines or handling crisis, if that pressure becomes the norm, it can lead to a level of distress that is debilitating in the short-term and, in the long-term, may contribute to a more permanent condition.

While stress may go with the job of managing, it is how you deal with the pressure that makes all the difference. Recognise the symptoms of stress as convincing data for change, find ways to relieve the daily work pressures, and plan to remove the longer term causes – you cannot kill time, but it can end up killing you.

REMEMBER

DO:

- Acknowledge your stress and recognise the symptoms as warning signals.

- Do something each day to relieve your short-term stress.

- Plan to take more care of your long-term stress through exercise or relaxation.

- Choose to manage your stress rather than be a victim – managing yourself includes managing your well being in the job.

Chapter 10

Start To Make It Happen

This chapter will help you to:

- plan for success in managing your time;
- appreciate the need to keep a healthy balance between your work and personal life;
- develop strategies and tactics for making better choices with time.

Start To Make It Happen

Do you ever wonder how some people achieve so much in their lives while others barely manage to survive? Do you sometimes wonder why some people make things happen while others wait for things to happen to them? Have you ever puzzled why some people are so successful in their careers and yet so unfulfilled in their personal lives? Although we attribute personal or job success to traits such as confidence, talent, money or charisma, most people who succeed in life do things to plan for their success and make time to work the plan: as the words of a recent song suggest: "It's not what you've got, it's what you do with what you've got."

PLAN FOR SUCCESS

Rather than lacking time to be effective, what most managers lack is direction and energy. While there are other avenues for getting direction, one place to start is with your ambitions and aspirations in your job. Although you may feel you are there to manage the day to day work and get results, you are also there to make things happen for the future, to change things, to develop things and to introduce new ideas – it is the leadership part of your function.

Write a short letter projecting yourself two years from now: What difference will you have made in your area? What will you have achieved, got done or made more time for in that period? Underline three things and make them commitments for action in the next six months. Put them up on the wall of your office as a reminder that you are not just there to do things but to achieve and get things done. Diarise an appointment with yourself three months from now to review progress on your long-term ambitions.

While most managers are comfortable with planning for today or for this week, they are less convinced about giving time to planning their long-term vision or goals. In the

WORD TO THE WISE
Nothing ventured, something lost.

same way that intending couples often give more time to planning the wedding than to planning the marriage, things go wrong for managers because they fail to anticipate and plan for the future. And long-term planning only happens if you make time in your diary to think about the business, to have off-site planning days or to set up a planning group.

Having plans is one thing, making them happen is another. Knowing where you are going for the future is important, but you cannot do a vision or a mission because they are too ambiguous and long-term. The way to work your long-term plan is to make those things into challenges and to fuel them with priorities and tasks in the shorter term. Combine your plans for the future with what you do on a daily and a weekly basis to ensure that you are going where you planned to go and to create energy and excitement for the journey.

GET MORE BALANCE IN YOUR LIFE

It is a fact that most managers today are working harder and longer hours than they did ten years ago. It is also a reality that many managers are experiencing job–related stress, taking little or no exercise, eating on the run and neglecting their personal lives.

On a tennis coaching holiday a couple of years ago, I met Peter who at coffee one morning began to tell me about a heart attack he had two years earlier. I found it hard to relate to the comment that it was the best thing that had ever happened to him. He explained that working long hours over several years had kept him away from his family to the extent that they did not seem to need or want him. Home became a less welcoming place and as a result he found even more convincing reasons to stay at the office. Regular visits from his family while he was recovering from triple bypass surgery gave him a second chance to appreciate what he was missing and a resolve to change his lifestyle. From believing that nothing would get done unless he was there to do it, he discovered that his staff were more than capable in his absence. He also came to realise that his job as manager was to provide them with leadership rather than with time.

To stay effective as a manager, it is important to maintain a good balance between your personal and work life. Rather than feeling guilty about the long hours or your lack of exercise, regard them as challenges to succeed in all aspects of your life. The following questions may help to clarify some of your personal aspirations over the next year.

- What are the main challenges in your personal life for the next year? Health, family, recreation, health, spirituality.

- Who is important in your life that you would like to give more time? Spouse, children, friends, parents, networks, clubs or societies.

- What childhood ambitions do you still harbour? Travel, relationships, hobby or interest.

- Have you a particular talent or skill you would like to develop? A language, acting, computer, voluntary or public speaking.

- Is there a decision you have put off in the last few months that you want to do something about? Weight, smoking, relationships, career, lifestyle or education.

- If you had a magic wand what would you change about your lifestyle?

> Take five minutes to list down all the things you would like to do something about in the next six months to get more balance into your life. Now pick two to focus on for the next month. Try making them into clear and measurable goals, for Example: Lose 6 lbs in weight by 31 December or plan four weekends away with the family and have two completed by 6 July.

PLAN AHEAD: ACT NOW

There is a big difference between having plans and making them happen. Action plans are no guarantee of action: most never get beyond the wish list stage. If you want to change your approach to your job or your personal life you need to treat them as overwhelming tasks that are best achieved by breaking them into bits and starting on the easy bits – remember that success breeds energy and energy breeds success. Many managers fail to realise their long-term ambitions or goals not because they lack direction but because they lose energy for the bigger challenges under pressure from the myriad of daily routines and minor problems.

If you seriously want to improve the way you manage your time, do not put this book down until you have resolved to do something in the next two weeks to start the process – any long journey begins with a single step. As a first step to improving your time management pick three things from the list below that you will absolutely commit to doing in the next two weeks.

- Go home earlier in the evenings.
- Block out one hour a week for planning.
- Delegate one responsibility to a staff member.
- Start keeping a daily 'to do' list.
- Only entertain staff problems if they have suggested solutions.
- Set monthly priorities and break them into managable tasks.
- Do up a weekly plan.
- Start tracking something you want to change, e.g. your hours.
- Stop taking work home.
- Schedule diary time to reset your monthly priorities.
- Delegate deadlines on longer tasks.
- Schedule half an hour a week for 'managing by wandering around'.
- Schedule one hour a week to blitz the paperwork, reading, etc.
- Redefine your role with your boss.
- Use discussion-enders with drop-ins.
- Hide for an hour a day or week.
- Work to the clock on big jobs.
- Start and finish all meetings on time.
- Time your telephone calls.

- Keep a time log.
- Get feedback on your bad habits from your staff.
- Do important things in your peak energy hour.
- Block out two hours in the next month to think about the business.
- Tackle one thing on which you have been pro-crastinating.
- Have a daily nap or quiet time.
- Take half an hour's walk in the evenings.
- Plan two events with family or friends this month.

Bring these commitments down onto your 'to do' list, weekly planner or diary, and when you have completed them choose another three until you start to see a difference. If you are having difficulty actioning any of the tasks consider breaking them into even smaller pieces or reflect on whether you really do want to change that particular piece of behaviour.

UNBLOCKING THE HABITS THAT KILL TIME

With the best of intentions many aspirations to change things in our lives come up against the force of habit, whether personal or organisational habits, sometimes called "culture". Start managing some of your bad habits by drawing up a list of the behaviours that get in the way of your personal effectiveness as a manager. It may help if you divide them into *personal* and *culture blocks*.

Personal	Culture
* Taking work home (A)	*Long hours (A)
Not saying no (A)	Open door policy

* Poor time planning *(A)*	*Instant response to customer queries
Over commitment (A)	* Meetings at peak energy time (A)

Refine the data on your personal and cultural habits by asterisking those which are the biggest blocks (*) – it is better to work on the major blockages than those which have less influence on your effectiveness. Also identify the actionability of each (A). There is no point trying to change things where you have no influence. Now plan to work on two of the big and actionable habits.

Break them into Bits

Treat your bad habits as baby elephants. You may not be able to tackle the whole problem but you could make a start on the easy bits. As part of the solution to poor time planning you could start with any of the following tasks.

- Keep a daily 'to do' list.
- Redefine your major priorities with your boss.
- Block out two hours for planning projects in your diary.
- Establish regular Monday meetings with your staff.
- Block out diary time for projects.
- Review your major projects for half an hour each Monday morning.

Replace Bad Habits with Good Ones

Identify a good habit that might encourage you to let go one of your bad habits. Most bad habits are difficult to tackle because they are chronic and we learn to live with them. One of the best ways of reversing bad habits is to replace them with something else, for example, get out of the habit of working long hours by scheduling one night a week for the cinema, theatre or a meal.

> The unfortunate thing about this world is that good habits are so much easier to give up than bad ones.
>
> Somerset Maughan

Get Support for Your Good Habits

One of the reasons some people never attempt to give up smoking or lose weight is the overwhelming fear of failure. We often talk ourselves into failing before we start – by using language such as "I have to", "I don't have a choice", "It's outside my control". Not only does negative dialogue drain your energy, but focusing on failure also blocks off the possibility of success.

> **WORD TO THE WISE**
> If you say you cannot do something, you are right, you cannot, because you have closed off to the possibility that you can.

Start building support for the habits you want to change by reversing the dialogue: "I can work less hours, I will plan my meetings better, I do have control on my commitments." Also get support from others by telling your boss or staff what you plan to do differently and ask them to nag and reward you for going home on time, setting monthly priorities or not giving in to specific time wasters.

Persist a Little Longer

A research study that compared successful and less successful managers suggests one important difference is that successful managers keep going a little longer. Weight watchers claim that it takes up to 31 days to break the habits of a lifetime, so give yourself time to succeed with your good habits. Make a commitment to doing one thing immediately (e.g. keeping a 'to do' list or having a quiet time in the day) and commit to it for at least three weeks: if it is not working by then, try something else. Like most things in this life, there is no right answer to changing your bad habits with time, just options that may or may not work in your particular circumstances. If you do not succeed with any one of the options, resist the temptation to label yourself a failure, see it as a challenge to succeed by doing something else.

Like all other organisational resources, time is there to be managed, and you start managing it by recognising that you do not have it completely under your control – some things you have to do and others are a choice. Commit yourself to making better choices with the time that is under your control by focusing on the important things whether daily, weekly or monthly and scheduling time for those things. Also, find creative ways to let go of the things that can so easily eat into your precious time or waste it. Even if you do not have staff to delegate the routine and urgency to, you can always delegate some of it into the wastepaper basket by giving it less time or not doing it at all.

Managing time is not a set of handy hints on how to be better organised – it is all too easy to be organised around the wrong things. Rather it is a process for making sure that you focus on the right things and put the time and energy where it belongs. Like most processes it is a journey that requires direction, energy and perseverance.

Hopefully this book has given you some guidelines and challenged some of the habits that may be blocking you from achieving what you want as a manager. And getting mileage from all the effort you are putting into the job is the reward for good self management – enjoy the journey.

REMEMBER

DO:

- Be aware that life is a journey not a destination – set aside time in the next month to plan the next stage of your journey.

- Three things in the next two weeks to action what you have learned or been reminded about in this book.

- Take more control of your time and yourself.

DO NOT:

- Let the job dictate your life – make time to maintain a healthy balance.

Further Reading

Further Reading

E C Bliss, *Getting Things Done, the ABC of Time Management* (London: Futura Books) 1985.

S R Covey & A R Merrill, *First Things First* (London: Simon & Schuster) 1994.

P Drucker, *The Effective Executive* (London: Pan Books) 1970.

H J Freudenberger & G Richardson, *Burnout* (London: Arrow Books) 1985.

W J Knaus, *Do it Now: How to Stop Procrastinating* (New York: Prentice-Hall) 1979.

A Lakien, *How to Get Control of your time and your Life* (England: Gower) 1984.

M Maltz, *Psycho-cybernetics* (Engelwood Cliffs: Wilshire Book Company) 1960.

R A Mackenzie, *The Time Trap* (New York: McGraw Hill) 1975.

M McCall & C A Segrist, *In Pursuit of the Manager's Job: Building on Mintzberg* (North Carolina, USA: Centre for Creative Leadership, Technical Report Number 14) 1980.

T McConalogue, "Real Delegation: The Art of Hanging On and Letting Go" *Management Decision* (1993) Vol. 31, No. 1, pp. 60-64.

T McConalogue, "Ten Tips for Time Management" *Management Magazine* (1996).

M McGannon, *The Urban Warriors Book of Solutions* (London: Pitman) 1996.

H Mintzberg, "The Managers Job: Folklore and Fact" *Harvard Business Review* (1975) 53,4.

W Oncken, *Managing Management Time* (New York: Prentice-Hall) 1984.

R G Rose, "Burnout" *Journal of Accountancy* (November 1986).

P Wilson, *Calm at Work* (London: Penguin Books) 1997.

For further information contact:

Tom McConalogue

Management and Organisation Development Consultant

32 Burlington Gardens

Dublin 4

Phone and Fax +353 (0)1 660 7312

11/6

Time sheets for week ⇒ job bags

Production list for 12 – 16.6

Initial criteria for meeting with KC